THE
50 TUDORS

THINGS YOU SHOULD KNOW ABOUT

Rupert Matthews

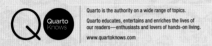

Quarto is the authority on a wide range of topics.
Quarto educates, entertains and enriches the lives of
our readers—enthusiasts and lovers of hands-on living.
www.quartoknows.com

Publisher: Maxime Boucknooghe
Editorial Director: Victoria Garrard
Art Director: Miranda Snow
Project Editor: Sophie Hallam
Design and Editorial: Tall Tree Ltd
Consultant: J.D.P. Cooper, Senior Lecturer
in History, University of York

Published in the United States by
QEB Publishing, Inc.
6 Orchard Road
Lake Forest, CA 92630

A CIP record for this book is available
from the Library of Congress.

ISBN 978 1 60992 963 3

Printed in China

Words in **bold** are explained
in the glossary on page 78.

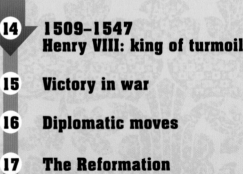

CONTENTS

INTRODUCTION

The Tudor era began with knights and castles, and ended with intercontinental trade and scientific discoveries, as the **medieval** period gave way to early modern times. England and Wales were profoundly changed between 1485 and 1603, with the Tudor monarchs transforming the religious, economic, social, and political life of the country.

AGE OF ADVENTURE

During the Tudor Age, Europeans discovered the Americas and found sea routes to Asia and East Africa. The Tudor monarchs encouraged English merchants to launch trading voyages to new lands, including Russia and India, while **Colonists** settled in North America. These ventures were the start of what was to become the British Empire.

◀ *The English explorer Sir Francis Drake being knighted by Queen Elizabeth I.*

RELIGION

When King Henry VII became king in 1485, England was part of a united Christian Europe led by the pope in Rome. By the time his granddaughter Elizabeth I died in 1603, England was a firmly **Protestant** nation at war with the **Catholic** powers. Religious disputes dominated European politics at this time.

▶ *The ruins of Fountains Abbey, closed by Henry VIII's religious reforms.*

GOVERNMENT

The chief advisors to King Henry VIII transformed the system of government. Before this time, the most important jobs had been held by the king's servants. Now, they were performed by government officials. **Parliament** became more important as the rulers sought the approval of their subjects for new taxes and laws.

Henry VIII (1491–1547)

▼ *England showed its growing military strength by defeating the Spanish Armada in 1588.*

LEISURE

During Tudor times, increasing wealth gave people more spare time. Many went to the theater to see works written by playwrights such as William Shakespeare. Others played sports, including tennis, soccer, and cricket.

▼ *The great Elizabethan playwright, William Shakespeare.*

MILITARY POWER

In the mid-15th century, England and Wales were torn apart by **civil war**, but the Tudors imposed unity. They transformed the military, bringing in new weapons and tactics. The Royal Navy was founded to keep warships ready for battle at all times. The defeat of the Spanish **Armada** in 1588 cemented England's reputation as a great military force.

1400–1485

The Welsh Tudors

The Tudors were a small land-owning family from North Wales. They rose to importance in the 15th-century **Wars of the Roses**, a vicious civil war between two branches of the royal family: the **House** of Lancaster (which included the Tudors) and the House of York. When the wars ended, a Tudor was on the throne, King Henry VII.

FAILED UPRISING

In 1400, the Tudors joined the **uprising** of the Welsh noble Owain Glyndwr against the English rule of Wales. After some initial success, the rebellion failed, leaving Meredith Tudor as the only survivor of the Tudor family. He had just one son, Owen, to inherit the Tudor name and history.

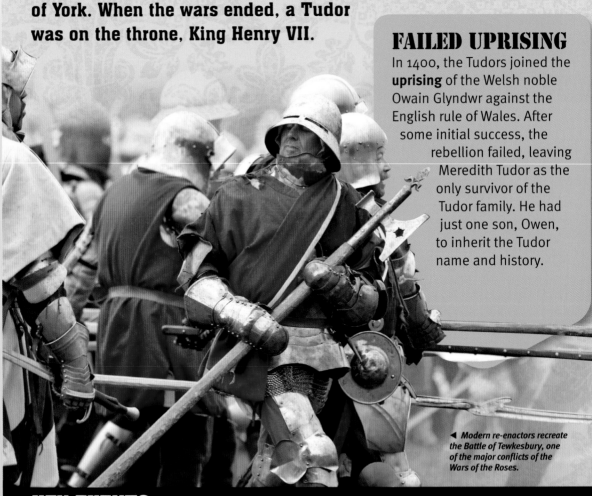

◄ *Modern re-enactors recreate the Battle of Tewkesbury, one of the major conflicts of the Wars of the Roses.*

KEY EVENTS

September 30, 1399
Henry IV becomes the first monarch from the House of Lancaster (see page 7).

1430 (date unknown)
Owen Tudor marries Catherine, the widow of Henry V (see page 8).

May 22, 1455
War breaks out between the houses of Lancaser and York (see page 10).

January 28, 1457
Owen Tudor's grandson, the future Henry VII, is born (see page 9).

LANCASTER VS. YORK

The houses of Lancaster and York were founded by the sons of Edward III (1312–77). His third son, John of Gaunt, was the first Duke of Lancaster, while his fourth son, Edmund, became the first Duke of York. The Lancastrians took control of the throne in 1399 when John's son became Henry IV. He was followed by his son, Henry V, who was followed by his son, Henry VI. However, Henry VI was such an unpopular leader that nobles began looking for someone to replace him from the House of York.

Henry VI (1421–71)

▼ Pembroke Castle in Wales, where Henry Tudor, later Henry VII, was born in 1457.

TUDOR LINKS

The Tudors' links to royalty also came through John of Gaunt. His second son, John, had a granddaughter who married into the Tudor family. This gave the Tudors a weak claim to the throne of England and Wales—which would get stronger over time.

◄ John of Gaunt (top row, second from the left), the first Duke of Lancaster, dines with the King of Portugal.

March 29, 1461	May 21, 1471	April 9, 1483	June 26 1483
Henry VI is defeated by the new king Edward IV at the Battle of Tewkesbury (see page 10).	Henry VI dies, leaving Henry Tudor as the main Lancastrian (see page 10).	Edward IV dies, passing the throne to his son, Edward V (see page 11).	Edward IV's brother seizes the throne to become Richard III (see page 11).

A royal marriage

It was Owen Tudor (1400–61) who made the Tudor family rich and influential. The son of a poor Welsh nobleman, he grew up to become a wealthy knight in England.

◄ *Henry V (1386–1422), the father of Henry VI and the husband of Catherine of Valois, who would later marry Owen Tudor.*

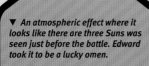

▼ *An atmospheric effect where it looks like there are three Suns was seen just before the battle. Edward took it to be a lucky omen.*

LUCKY ACCIDENT

At the age of about 20, Owen got a job working at the English royal **court** for the noble Baron Hungerford. One evening, in 1427, Owen was dancing at court when he tripped and fell into the lap of a lady. She was Queen Catherine, the 26-year-old widow of King Henry V and mother of King Henry VI. Owen Tudor and Catherine fell in love and were married in 1430.

A BLOODY DEATH

During the Wars of the Roses, Owen Tudor fought with his stepson King Henry VI against Edward of York. In 1461, he led the Lancastrian troops to defeat at the Battle of Mortimer's Cross. Afterward, he was executed and his head put on display as a warning to other would-be rebels.

THE CHILDREN

Owen Tudor and Queen Catherine had three children who survived to become adults. Edward, born 1432, became a monk. Jasper, born 1431, became Earl of Pembroke and later married Catherine Woodville, sister to the wife of King Edward IV. Edmund, born 1430, was made Earl of Richmond by his royal half-brother King Henry VI—his son would go on to found the Tudor **dynasty** as Henry VII.

▼ *Owen Tudor's coat of arms represents the three lords killed in battle by his 13th-century ancestor, Ednyfed Fychan.*

The Beaufort claim

Margaret Beaufort (1443–1509)

As half-brothers to King Henry VI, Edmund and Jasper Tudor led privileged lives with connections to many noble families. A marriage would bring the Tudors even closer to the throne of England.

THE MARRIAGE

In 1455, Edmund Tudor married Margaret Beaufort, daughter of John Beaufort, the Duke of Somerset. The next year, Edmund was captured by Yorkist forces and imprisoned in Wales, where he died of the plague. Margaret gave birth to their son, Henry Tudor, just a few months later.

KEEPING WATCH

The new king Edward IV felt he should keep a watch on his possible rival for the throne. So, in 1461 he ordered Margaret to hand over the four-year-old Henry, who was sent to live with a man loyal to Edward. But when Henry VI retook the throne in 1470, Henry was brought back to court. However, he was forced to flee the country the next year after the **restoration** of Edward IV.

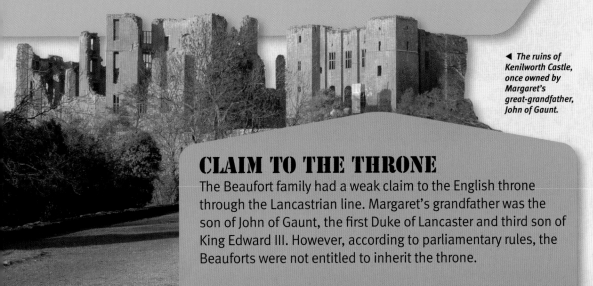

◄ *The ruins of Kenilworth Castle, once owned by Margaret's great-grandfather, John of Gaunt.*

CLAIM TO THE THRONE

The Beaufort family had a weak claim to the English throne through the Lancastrian line. Margaret's grandfather was the son of John of Gaunt, the first Duke of Lancaster and third son of King Edward III. However, according to parliamentary rules, the Beauforts were not entitled to inherit the throne.

Margaret Beaufort was 12 years old at the time of her marriage to Edmund Tudor.

The Wars of the Roses

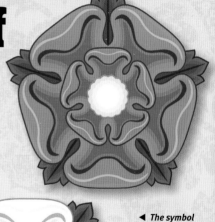

King Henry VI was a weak ruler who had allowed **corruption** to spread. When he fell sick, many nobles wanted Richard, Duke of York to replace him. Fighting between the two sides broke out in 1455. Richard was killed in 1460, so his son Edward took over the Yorkist cause.

◄ *The symbol of Lancaster was a red rose, while York was represented by a white one, hence the Wars of the Roses.*

▲ *Edward of York (right) leads the fighting at the bloody Battle of Towton.*

TOWTON

The war lasted from 1455 to 1487. The largest battle ever fought in England took place in 1461 at Towton, in Yorkshire. There were about 35,000 men on each side, and 28,000 died. Henry VI's army was defeated, and Edward of York became King of England as Edward IV.

◄ *A mace, or metal club, from the time of the Wars of the Roses.*

TEWKESBURY

In 1470, a rebellion broke out against King Edward IV. The king defeated his enemies at the Battle of Tewkesbury in 1471. Both Henry VI and his son, Edward, died. That left Henry Tudor as the only Lancastrian claimant to the throne.

▲ *A 15th-century two-handed long sword.*

Soldiers wore armor into battle and fought using swords, axes, clubs, and bows.

The princes in the tower

When Edward IV died in 1483, his 12-year-old son was proclaimed King Edward V. Owing to his young age, his uncle, Richard, ruled on his behalf, while Edward and his younger brother were sent to live in the Tower of London.

Richard III (1452–85)

THE PRINCES VANISH

Soon into Edward V's reign, Edward IV's marriage to Elizabeth Woodville was declared to have been invalid. This meant that Edward V was **illegitimate** and not entitled to be king. Richard took the throne for himself, ruling as Richard III. The princes in the tower vanished soon after. Many historians believe they were murdered on Richard III's orders.

▶ A romantic depiction of the princes by the 19th-century French artist Paul Delaroche.

THE IMPOSTER

Years later, when Henry Tudor was king, a young man claimed that he was Richard of York, one of the vanished princes. He tried to seize the throne but was defeated and executed by Henry, who said he was an imposter called Perkin Warbeck.

In 1674, workmen in the tower found a buried box containing two small skeletons.

1485–1509

Henry VII: prince of peace

When Henry Tudor became king, few people knew much about him. He had lived abroad for 15 years, hiding from possible assassins from England. In fact, as he had spent only a few weeks at the English court in 1470, few nobles had even met him. Nobody knew if he would be able to rule a kingdom as large and as troubled as England.

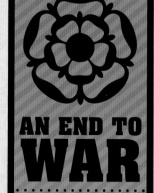

AN END TO WAR

Henry's first aim was to end the Wars of the Roses. He made sure that anyone with a possible claim to the throne either supported him or was dead. He also used legal trickery to punish those who were hostile to him, and took away the power of nobles to form their own armies.

Elizabeth of York (1466–1503)

Henry VII (1457–1509)

When in exile, Henry Tudor was so poor that he borrowed money to buy food.

KEY EVENTS

1471
Henry Tudor is sent to live in Brittany for his own safety (see page 14).

August 22, 1485
Henry defeats Richard III at the Battle of Bosworth to become King Henry VII (see page 15).

January 18, 1486
Henry VII's marriage unites the houses of Lancaster and York (see page 16).

June 16, 1487
A rebellion against Henry is defeated at Stoke Field (see page 17).

◀ *A gold coin known as an "angel" from the reign of Henry VII. Its name comes from its depiction of the archangel Michael slaying a dragon.*

PROSPERITY

Henry found that the English government was almost bankrupt. He brought in new coins, new taxes, and more efficient ways of making sure everyone paid their taxes. He was often accused of being greedy, but he gradually brought England back to prosperity.

FOREIGN TREATIES

Henry knew that wars cost a lot of money and stopped trade, so he fought few wars. Instead he set about making **treaties** and increasing trade. Many people in England thought he gave away too much in these treaties, but Henry believed that peace was worth the price he paid.

▲ *Henry negotiated treaties with several foreign rulers, including the powerful King of Aragon, Ferdinand II, pictured here.*

◀ *Henry's careful management of his wealth allowed him to leave a large sum in his will to pay for the building of a new chapel at Westminster Abbey.*

February 24, 1496
Henry signs the *Intercursus Magnus*, a major trading treaty (see page 18).

April 2, 1502
Henry's eldest son Arthur dies, leaving his brother Henry as heir (see page 23).

August 8, 1503
Henry's daughter marries James IV of Scotland (see page 20).

April 21, 1509
Henry dies of tuberculosis aged 52 (see page 23).

Henry in exile

▼ Pembroke Castle in West Wales.

Henry Tudor's early life was spent under constant threat from his Yorkist rivals. When he was just 13 years old, his uncle decided to take him to live abroad for his own safety.

ROYAL ANCESTRY

Henry was born in Pembroke Castle in 1457. His father, Edmund Tudor, had died three months earlier. He was brought up in luxury by his father's brother, Jasper Tudor. Henry was the great-great grandson of John of Gaunt, the Duke of Lancaster, the third son of King Edward III. During the Wars of the Roses, so many of Henry's relatives were killed that he ended up as one of the few descendants of John of Gaunt still alive and able to claim the throne. This meant he was constantly under threat from rivals.

LIFE ABROAD

In 1470, Jasper Tudor fled to Brittany to avoid being executed by Edward IV, taking the 13-year-old Henry Tudor with him. Henry lived with Duke Francis II of Brittany, who thought a man with a claim to the English throne would be a useful tool in **diplomacy**. Francis kept Henry in comfort but as a virtual prisoner for the next 14 years.

Henry Stafford (1454–83)

FAILED INVASION

In 1483, Henry made his first attempt to seize the English throne. Having gained the support of the powerful noble Henry Stafford, Henry hired soldiers to invade England. However, a storm forced Henry's ships back to Brittany, while Stafford was caught and beheaded by Richard III.

The Battle of Bosworth

In 1485, Henry Tudor decided to try to invade England again. He had the support of King Charles VIII of France and hoped that by working with rebel English nobles he could defeat Richard III. When they met at the Battle of Bosworth, Henry emerged the winner.

◄ The coat of arms of Henry VII.

◄ The coat of arms of Richard III.

▼ Richard III fights off an attacker during the Battle of Bosworth. He was later killed in the battle.

Richard III's remains were discovered in 2012, buried beneath a parking lot in Leicester.

MARCH TO BOSWORTH

Henry Tudor landed in west Wales with a small army of French soldiers. He recruited Welshmen to his cause, then linked up with English nobles. Richard marched to Leicester to try to block Henry's route to London. The two armies met near Market Bosworth, just outside Leicester.

THE BATTLE

The battle began soon after dawn as Henry advanced to attack Richard. Richard's army numbered 10,000 men, far more than Henry's 5000. But an area of marsh prevented part of Richard's army from joining the fighting. Neither side could get an advantage until Lord Stanley, who was married to Henry's mother, entered the battle late on with his 6000 men. It swung the conflict in Henry's favor. Richard died fighting, suffering 11 wounds to his head.

Securing the throne

By the time he became king, Henry had already lived through the reigns of three other monarchs. Henry VI had been murdered, Edward IV had died of disease and Richard III had been killed in battle. Henry was determined to lead a long life, which meant he had to secure his throne.

OATH

Henry cleverly announced that his reign had officially begun the day before the Battle of Bosworth. That meant anyone who had not supported him before then was a **traitor**. But he said they would be forgiven if they took an oath of loyalty. Men flocked to take the oath.

RIGHT OF MIGHT

Henry's right to the throne was weak. Other men had equally strong claims. He therefore declared that the throne was his by "right of conquest," not by "right of inheritance" (who he was related to). This meant that nobody could challenge his right to rule in a court of law or in Parliament.

A SAFE MARRIAGE

In January 1486, Henry married Elizabeth of York, eldest daughter of King Edward IV. This meant that the Yorkist claim to the throne would pass to his own children. To make sure there were no rival heirs, he also married the younger sisters of Elizabeth of York to some of his closest supporters.

▶ *Stained-glass window in Cardiff Castle of Henry VII and his wife.*

Henry VII passed a law in 1486 banning nobles from having their own armies.

Henry used a new badge, the Tudor Rose. This combined the white rose of York with the red rose of Lancaster to symbolize the joining of the two royal families. Henry took care not to use other symbols of either side in the Wars of the Roses. The new badge was supposed to mark a new beginning for England.

IN PRISON

Within days of the Battle of Bosworth, Henry arrested anyone who might cause trouble. This included the ten-year-old Edward, Earl of Warwick, the nephew of Edward IV and Richard III. Warwick was thrown in prison where he was executed 15 years later.

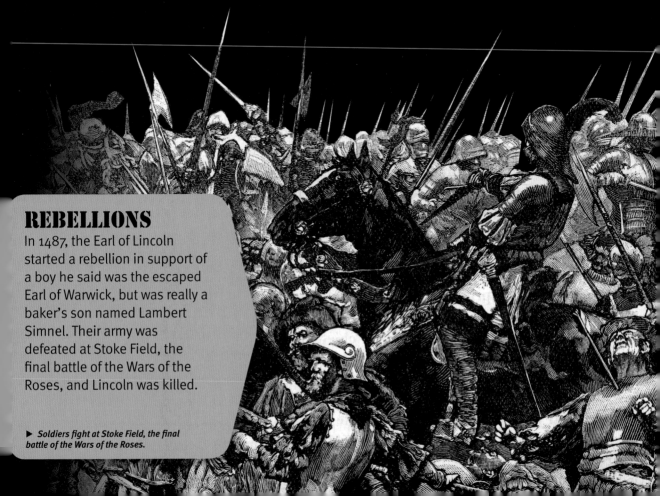

REBELLIONS

In 1487, the Earl of Lincoln started a rebellion in support of a boy he said was the escaped Earl of Warwick, but was really a baker's son named Lambert Simnel. Their army was defeated at Stoke Field, the final battle of the Wars of the Roses, and Lincoln was killed.

▶ Soldiers fight at Stoke Field, the final battle of the Wars of the Roses.

The wealth of England

Henry Tudor had no experience of running the finances of a kingdom, or even of being a wealthy landowner. He had to learn how to run a country once he was already king. He took over an England made poor by years of warfare, and left it wealthy and prosperous.

INTERCURSUS MAGNUS

In 1496, Henry signed a treaty known as *Intercursus Magnus* with a number of important trading areas, including the Duchy of Burgundy, Venice, Florence, and the Holy Roman Empire. The treaty lowered the duties that had to be paid by merchants moving goods between countries.

A ROYAL FORTUNE

When Henry became King of England, the royal **treasury** was empty. By carefully spending less money than earlier kings, he managed to save a vast fortune. When he died, he left £1.25 million to his son, Henry VIII—more than $1 billion in today's money.

COINAGE

Henry also changed the money being used in England. In 1489, he introduced a coin containing half an ounce of gold, the sovereign. He also fixed the silver content in silver coins at 92.5 percent pure silver so that everyone knew how much a coin was really worth.

▲ *A silver groat (a coin worth 4 pence) from Henry VII's reign, bearing the king's likeness.*

RISING POPULATION

The number of people in England rose quickly during Henry's reign. It is thought that in 1475 there were about two million people living there, but by 1510 that had risen to nearly three million. The growing population put pressure on land, but also provided cheap labor for new businesses.

▼ *With a rising population, London became increasingly built up in the Tudor age, as this engraving from 1545 shows.*

VAGABONDS

Henry agreed to the Vagabond **Act** in 1495, which made it illegal to beg for money. Instead, poor people were sent to the monasteries to ask for food or shelter. Richer people donated money to help the poor, mostly through monasteries or churches who administered the funds.

▲ *A 1536 woodcut showing a vagabond being punished.*

THE WOOL TRADE

England's wool was considered to be some of the best in Europe. Large quantities were exported, bringing wealth to the country. During Henry's reign, more and more wool was dyed and woven into cloth in England before it was exported, increasing the profits made by English merchants and providing more jobs for workers.

Making peace

Wars cost a lot of money, so Henry Tudor was eager to keep the peace with England's neighboring countries. However, disputes meant he had to work very hard at peace— and did not always succeed.

▲ *Charles VIII's coat of arms.*

PEACE WITH FRANCE

When Henry became king, England was still technically at war with France. Edward IV had agreed to a truce in 1475, but this was not a permanent peace. In 1492, Henry threatened to invade France unless a settlement was reached.

King Charles VIII of France at once agreed to sign the Treaty of Etaples and to pay Henry 50,000 gold crowns a year for the next 15 years.

SCOTLAND

England had fought many wars with Scotland. In 1502, Henry agreed the Treaty of Perpetual Peace with Scotland's King James IV. James also married Henry's daughter Margaret, so future Scottish monarchs would be linked to the English royal family.

King James IV (1473–1513)

PEACE WITH SPAIN

In previous years, the English had sent armies to fight in Spanish civil wars. The Treaty of Medina del Campo in 1489 brought peace, with the countries also agreeing to help each other if either were attacked by France. It was arranged for Henry's eldest son, Arthur, to marry King Ferdinand II's daughter, Catherine. Both children were under five years old, so they didn't wed until 1501.

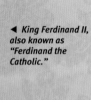

◄ *King Ferdinand II, also known as "Ferdinand the Catholic."*

James IV was originally going to marry Cecily, the daughter of Edward IV.

◀ *Anne, the Duchess of Britanny.*

HOLY ROMAN EMPIRE

This empire covered what is now Germany, Switzerland, Netherlands, Belgium, Austria, the Czech Republic, and parts of Poland, Italy, and France. It was a loose group of different countries rather than a united **state**. When Henry became king, Emperor Maximilian I was fighting a war in Italy and was trying to reform his own empire. He quickly agreed to a treaty with Henry that improved trade between England and the empire.

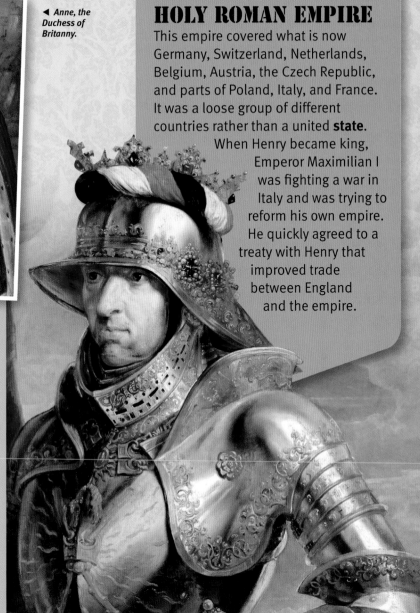

WAR IN BRITTANY

In Tudor times, Brittany was an independent country in France ruled by Duke Francis II. Francis agreed to let his daughter, Anne, marry an English nobleman, the Duke of Buckingham, loyal to Henry VII. In return, Henry promised that the English army would protect Brittany from any French invasion. But before the wedding could take place, Francis died and King Charles VIII of France invaded Brittany. After months of bitter fighting, Charles captured Anne and forced her to marry him instead of Buckingham.

▶ *Emperor Maximilian I wearing his royal armor.*

PAPAL SUPPORT

The pope in Rome was the leader of the Church all across Western Europe, and a powerful figure. Henry persuaded the then pope, Innocent VIII, to **excommunicate** anyone who rebelled against his rule.

▶ *Pope Innocent VIII*

Law and order

The long Wars of the Roses left England with gangs of bandits roaming around the countryside, while nobles fought private feuds and refused to obey the laws of the king. Henry was determined to impose order on England.

◀ Examples of a standardized Tudor weight (left) and carpenter's ruler (below).

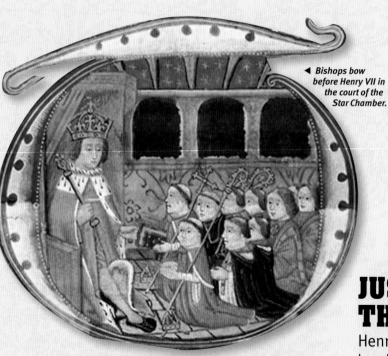

◀ Bishops bow before Henry VII in the court of the Star Chamber.

WEIGHTS AND MEASURES

In 1494 and 1496, Henry passed new laws concerning the weights and measures used in shops and businesses. These ensured that the same-sized measures were used throughout England, abolishing local customs that could cause confusion when goods were traded from one area to another. The rules were enforced by the justices of the peace.

JUSTICES OF THE PEACE

Henry increased the power of local justices of the peace (JPs). These men were local landowners or merchants whose job was to preserve the "King's Peace" by punishing lawbreakers. They could impose fines or other punishments and could use armed men to back up their decisions. A JP was appointed for one year at a time, and served without being paid.

THE STAR CHAMBER

Nobles accused of crimes could bully local judges and men serving on juries. So, in 1487, Henry founded the Star Chamber. This was a special court in London that tried nobles who might escape justice in their local areas. Henry used the Star Chamber to impose heavy fines on nobles who broke the law.

Prince Arthur

Henry and his queen Elizabeth had seven children: three sons and four daughters. The eldest son and **heir** was Arthur, born in 1486. Arthur's sudden death in 1502 plunged Henry into grief and the Tudor family into crisis.

▼ *The ruins of Ludlow Castle where Arthur, Prince of Wales, died at age 15 in 1502.*

Trained to be king, Arthur was given the best education available. He was named in honor of the legendary King Arthur to show that the Tudors were an ancient family and rightful rulers of England.

◄ *Prince Arthur portrayed in a stained-glass window created shortly before his death.*

MARRIAGE AND SUDDEN DEATH

Prince Arthur finally married Catherine of Aragon in 1501 when they were both 15. After the wedding, they moved to Wales. In March 1502, the couple began suffering from an unknown illness. Within days Arthur was dead, though Catherine recovered.

THE KING'S SLOW DEMISE

After dealing with the tragedy of his son death, Henry was dealt a further blow the following year with the death of his wife, Elizabeth. Henry's final years saw him enter a slow decline. He died of tuberculosis in 1509.

After his wife died in 1503, Henry VII locked himself in a room for six weeks.

1509–1547

Henry VIII: king of turmoil

The new king, Henry VIII, was young, handsome, and popular. He was very unlike his old, miserly, and sickly father. Everyone hoped the new reign would be a time of glory and prosperity. But things soon started to go wrong. Henry turned into a bad-tempered tyrant and England's economy went into decline.

◄ *Slim and sporty when young, Henry put on a lot of weight in the last decade of his life.*

Henry was highly educated. At age 10, he could speak Latin, French, and Italian.

HENRY'S ILLNESSES

When he was young, Henry was very fit. However, after he was nearly killed in a jousting accident in 1536, he suffered almost permanent illness and crippling pain. His mind may have been affected by the injuries as well since he became increasingly vicious, bad-tempered, and violent.

KEY EVENTS

June 1520
Henry meets the French king at the Field of Cloth of Gold (see page 27).

May 23, 1533
Henry's first marriage to Catherine of Aragon is annulled (see page 31).

November 11, 1534
Henry becomes head of the Church of England (see page 31).

January 24, 1536
Henry is seriously injured while jousting (see page 40).

SIX WIVES

Church law forbade men from marrying their brother's widow. But Henry received permission from the pope to wed Catherine of Aragon, his brother Arthur's widow. His search for a son to inherit his throne led Henry to marry six times.

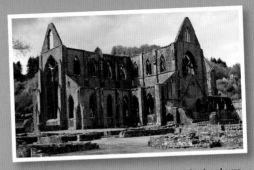

▲ The ruins of Tintern Abbey, which was forced to hand over its estates to the king during the destruction of the monasteries.

▲ The six wives of Henry VIII. Top row, from left: Catherine of Aragon, Anne Boleyn, Jane Seymour. Bottom row: Anne of Cleves, Catherine Howard, Catherine Parr.

RELIGION IN CRISIS

Religion underwent a revolution under Henry's rule. In Europe, new religious ideas split Christians into two camps: Catholics and Protestants. Henry began by strongly supporting Catholicism. But his later marriage troubles changed his mind, and led him to break from the pope's authority and establish a new Church of England.

MONEY AND POWER

England's economy suffered under Henry, causing widespread poverty. Henry launched costly foreign wars, but gained little for the vast sums he spent. Changes to the workings of government made the kingdom more efficient, but reduced the monarchy's powers.

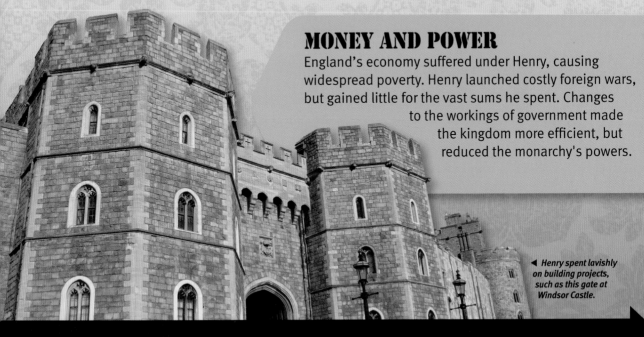

◄ Henry spent lavishly on building projects, such as this gate at Windsor Castle.

1536
Henry begins seizing the monasteries' wealth (see pages 32–33).

October 12, 1537
Henry's third wife gives birth to his only son, Edward (see page 38).

July 12, 1543
Henry marries for the sixth and final time to Catherine Parr (see page 39).

January 28, 1547
Henry dies, leaving the throne to his nine-year-old son, Edward (see page 43).

Victory in war

Henry VII had avoided wars as they were very expensive. But Henry VIII dreamed of achieving personal glory in battle and of regaining England's lost territories in France. At the first opportunity, he went to war.

WAR WITH FRANCE

In 1511, Henry sent troops to join a Spanish invasion of France, but it failed. Two years later, Henry led his own army to invade northern France, where he won the Battle of the Spurs and captured the cities of Tournai and Thérouanne. A larger campaign was planned for 1514, but Henry called it off due to the high costs.

WARFARE

A new form of warfare was becoming common in Henry VIII's reign. Large guns had been around for more than 100 years, but now smaller guns were being used by soldiers instead of swords, pikes, and bows. Most men stopped wearing full suits of armor as they couldn't stop bullets, though some continued to wear helmets and breastplates.

◄ *One of Henry VIII's full suits of armor.*

◄ *King James IV lies dying at the Battle of Flodden.*

WAR WITH SCOTLAND

When Henry VIII invaded France, the French king called on King James IV of Scotland to honor the Franco-Scottish alliance and attack England. Scottish troops invaded England where they were attacked by an English army at Flodden. King James was killed along with most of his men. Scotland made peace.

Diplomatic moves

Despite his love of military glory, Henry VIII realized it was cheaper to talk to the rulers of other countries than to fight them. As his reign went on, he began to use diplomacy more and more to achieve his aims.

THE TREATY OF LONDON

In the early 16th century, the Muslim Ottoman Empire had conquered several Christian states in eastern Europe. To try to curb this threat, Henry signed a treaty with other European states, agreeing not to fight each other. The peace did not last long.

▶ *During the rule of Suleiman I (1520–66), the Ottoman Empire reached its peak, stretching across much of eastern and central Europe.*

LORD OF IRELAND

Henry inherited the title of Lord of Ireland, and ruled lands near Dublin. Although the other Irish lords had accepted him as their superior, they rarely did as he told them. In 1542, he persuaded the Irish Parliament to make him King of Ireland, but most Irish lords continued to ignore his instructions.

◀ *A 1545 painting of the Field of Cloth of Gold. Despite its splendor, the meeting achieved little as Henry and Francis argued soon after.*

THE FIELD OF CLOTH OF GOLD

In June 1520, Henry VIII met Francis I of France in Calais at a huge festival lasting more than two weeks. Each monarch tried to outdo the other with lavish entertainment. So much cloth made from silk and gold wire was used that the event was named the Field of Cloth of Gold.

In 1529, Ottoman armies reached Vienna in Austria, but failed to capture the city.

The Reformation

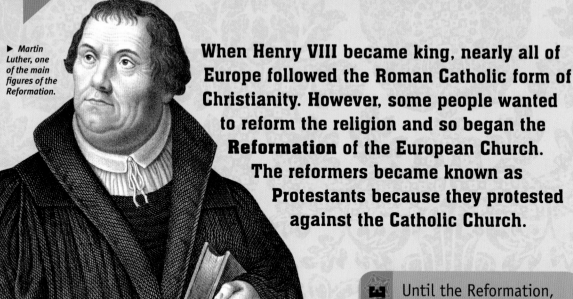

▶ *Martin Luther, one of the main figures of the Reformation.*

When Henry VIII became king, nearly all of Europe followed the Roman Catholic form of Christianity. However, some people wanted to reform the religion and so began the **Reformation** of the European Church. The reformers became known as Protestants because they protested against the Catholic Church.

MARTIN LUTHER

In 1517, a friar named Martin Luther wrote a list of things he thought were wrong with the Catholic Church. He nailed his "95 Theses" to the church door in Wittenberg, Germany, so that people could read them. In 1521, Pope Leo X expelled Luther from the Church. But Luther went on to translate the Bible into German, allowing ordinary people to read the scriptures for themselves for the first time.

PAPAL RULE

Until the Reformation, people believed that only the pope could decide what the Bible really meant—it was written in Latin, a language most people couldn't understand. The rulings of popes had a huge influence on how people lived.

BY FAITH ALONE

The Catholic Church taught that people could be forgiven for sins if they undertook good works such as helping the poor. Protestants said that only God could forgive sins. They believed people would be forgiven for their sins if they displayed true faith in God.

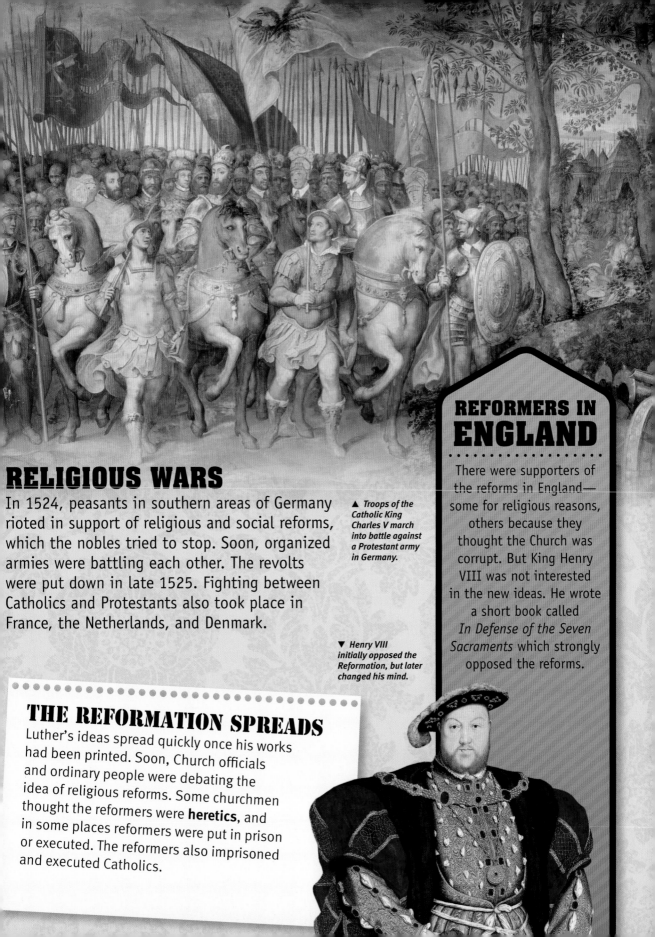

RELIGIOUS WARS

In 1524, peasants in southern areas of Germany rioted in support of religious and social reforms, which the nobles tried to stop. Soon, organized armies were battling each other. The revolts were put down in late 1525. Fighting between Catholics and Protestants also took place in France, the Netherlands, and Denmark.

▲ Troops of the Catholic King Charles V march into battle against a Protestant army in Germany.

▼ Henry VIII initially opposed the Reformation, but later changed his mind.

THE REFORMATION SPREADS

Luther's ideas spread quickly once his works had been printed. Soon, Church officials and ordinary people were debating the idea of religious reforms. Some churchmen thought the reformers were **heretics**, and in some places reformers were put in prison or executed. The reformers also imprisoned and executed Catholics.

The king's "Great Matter"

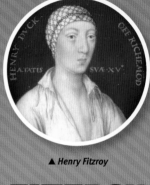

▲ *Henry Fitzroy*

By 1525, Henry VIII had begun to worry about his dynasty. He had a daughter but no sons or brothers, and his two sisters had married foreign rulers. Henry decided that having an heir was an urgent priority.

Anne Boleyn had been maid of honor to the wife of French king Francis I.

FITZROY

Henry did have an illegitimate son, Henry Fitzroy, and it was suggested that the king could make him his heir. Another suggestion was to arrange a future marriage for his then nine-year-old daughter, Mary, so she could have a son in the future. But Henry turned down both ideas.

ANNE BOLEYN

In February 1526, Henry met and fell in love with a young noblewoman named Anne Boleyn. Henry decided he wanted to marry Anne, but couldn't do so unless he could annul his existing marriage to Catherine of Aragon.

▶ *Hever Castle, where Anne Boleyn spent her youth.*

Catherine of Aragon (1485–1536)

ANNULMENT

Divorce was forbidden by the Catholic Church at this time, so Henry told his chief minister Cardinal Wolsey to arrange an **annulment**. This meant convincing the pope that the marriage was illegal and should never have taken place in the first place because Henry should not have been given permission to marry his brother's widow.

THE POPE'S PROBLEM

When Pope Clement VII received Henry's request for an annulment, he was a prisoner of Holy Roman Emperor Charles V —Catherine of Aragon's nephew. He could not, therefore, grant the annulment, but he did not want to anger Henry by refusing outright. Instead he found a series of excuses to delay making a decision.

A NEW QUEEN

Pressured by Henry, Thomas Cranmer, the Archbishop of Canterbury, organized a court of English Church officials in 1533. Meeting without the permission of the pope, it decided that Henry's marriage to Catherine was illegal. A week later Anne Boleyn was crowned queen, and soon after she gave birth to a daughter, Elizabeth.

▶ Anne Boleyn was just 23 years old when Henry met and fell in love with her.

▲ Pope Clement VII

THE ACT OF SUPREMACY

In 1534, the English Parliament passed an Act of Supremacy. This made Henry head of the Church in England, removing all authority from the pope. Pope Clement responded by excommunicating Henry and Cranmer. Henry was now supreme ruler of the state and the Church in England.

31

The end of the monasteries

As the new head of the Church in England, Henry VIII decided to use some of the Church's wealth to pay his bills. This, along with the Reformation, led to a massive reorganization of the English Church. The main target was the monasteries.

MONASTIC ENGLAND

In 1535, there were 900 religious houses in England. More than one percent of the country's population was leading a religious life as a monk or nun, and about 25 percent of all land belonged to these religious houses. The monasteries also cared for the poor and provided education for some children.

THE VISITATION

Henry's new chief minister, Thomas Cromwell, sent out teams of officials to visit all the monasteries. They had two tasks: to assess the monasteries for taxation and to see if the monks were doing their jobs properly. They reported that a number of monasteries were not following the rules, and that many monks were living luxurious lives and not conducting religious services properly.

FIRST SUPPRESSION

As a result of Cromwell's survey, 243 of the smaller religious houses were closed in 1536. Their property was then transferred to the **Crown**. The monks were given a choice of moving to another monastery or of taking a sum of cash and leaving the Church.

▶ *The ruins of Furness Abbey in Cumbria, which closed in 1537.*

▼ *Pro-monastery protesters take to the streets of York during the Pilgrimage of Grace.*

THE PILGRIMAGE OF GRACE

In October 1536, a riot broke out in Louth, Lincolnshire, when the local abbey was closed down. The unrest spread and soon 40,000 men were occupying the city of York, demanding that the closure of monasteries stop. They called themselves the "Pilgrimage of Grace." The government compromised and the "pilgrims" went home. But when a new rising took place in 1537, Henry ordered the execution of more than 200 men.

WASTED WEALTH

The huge rents paid on land formerly owned by the monasteries now went to the king. At first it was intended that the land would be kept by the king to provide him with regular income, but Henry later sold most of the land and spent the cash.

THE SECOND SUPPRESSION

By 1538, Cromwell had decided to close down all the monasteries. Abbots and monks were encouraged to dissolve their own monasteries by being given generous pensions and cash payments. Nearly all the monasteries volunteered to close down. Those that did not were shut down by the king's officials.

The king's ministers

When Henry VIII came to the throne, the system of government in England was little different from that of the medieval monarchs. But by the time he died, this had been replaced by a system that was more like that of the modern world.

THE PERSONAL STATE

In theory, the entire kingdom and everything in it belonged to the monarch, and the king could do whatever he liked. In practice, the monarch needed the support of the nobles, merchants, and Church. All kings had to follow established customs and laws if they were to persuade others to do what they wanted.

▼ When Wolsey fell from favor in 1529, Henry seized his lavish palace, Hampton Court.

CARDINAL WOLSEY

Henry made Cardinal Thomas Wolsey, Archbishop of York, his **lord chancellor** in 1515. Wolsey sent out officials to find out exactly how rich the country's nobles and merchants were. This allowed him to tax the nobles more and the lower classes less. Wolsey also made it cheaper and easier for people to take cases to court, allowing poorer people to get justice if they were mistreated by the rich.

◄ Thomas Wolsey wearing his cardinal's robes.

SIR THOMAS MORE

Wolsey was stripped of his offices and wealth in 1529 for failing to get the pope to annul Henry's first marriage. The scholar and lawyer Sir Thomas More took his place as lord chancellor. Although he was an able minister, he was a firm Catholic and refused to accept Henry as head of the Church in England. In 1532, he resigned. Three years later Henry had him tried for treason and executed.

Sir Thomas More
(1478–1535)

THOMAS CROMWELL

Born the son of a London blacksmith, Cromwell rose to become the second most powerful man in England when he was appointed royal secretary. He introduced major reforms to the state, making sure that the most important jobs were now carried out by government officials rather than the king's servants. This made the government more efficient, though it meant that the king had less power over how it worked.

LORD THOMAS AUDLEY

The act of Parliament that sent Cromwell to his death was organized by Sir Thomas Audley, who took over as lord chancellor. Audley introduced no serious reforms during his time in office.

CROMWELL'S FALL

It was Thomas Cromwell who persuaded Henry VIII to marry Anne of Cleves. When that marriage went wrong (see page 39), Henry became angry with Cromwell. Cromwell was arrested in June 1540, and Henry asked Parliament to declare his former secretary a traitor. Cromwell was executed without trial, but within weeks, Henry regretted his death.

"Old Coppernose"

Henry VIII and family

▲ Henry and his court were always dressed in the finest, most expensive clothes, as this 19th-century picture shows.

Henry VIII inherited a fortune from his father but wasted it all on luxurious living and wars. Even worse, his bad financial decisions ruined the economy. Henry tried to get rich by ordering silver coins to be made mostly of copper with just a thin silver coating. People noticed that the silver soon rubbed off the nose of Henry's portrait on the coins. They began calling Henry "Old Coppernose."

POVERTY

During Henry's reign, the number of poor people grew. There were fewer jobs to be found and wages for unskilled workers fell. The rich were expected to help poor people through charity, but the increasing numbers of people without work made this difficult.

▼ St James's Palace in London, one of several palaces built or enlarged by Henry.

VAST EXPENSE

Henry not only spent vast sums of money buying the latest weapons and fighting wars, he also built lavish palaces for himself and his family. In all, he owned more than 50 palaces and houses. They cost him a fortune.

Henry had a stable of 200 horses and owned more than 2000 fine tapestries.

The Royal Navy

At the start of Henry VIII's reign, the English navy was made up of just a handful of small ships. Over the next few decades, Henry created one of the most powerful naval fleets in the world, with more than 50 big warships.

NEW SHIPS

Henry established royal dockyards at Chatham and Woolwich. Here a new type of warship was built, which used guns to attack enemy ships. Previous ships had relied on getting close to other ships, and either ramming them or using their crew to board them.

▶ A wooden Tudor tankard used on one of Henry VIII's new ships.

THE ADMIRALTY

In 1546, Henry founded the Admiralty. This organization looked after the administration of the navy. It supervised the building and arming of ships, and ensured that there were always enough ships to deal with an emergency. The Admiralty still exists today.

▲ In 1545, the warship Mary Rose was sunk in a battle with the French. It was brought back to the surface in 1982.

◀ Henry's coastal fort at St Mawes in Cornwall still stands.

COASTAL FORTS

As well as expanding and improving the navy, Henry ordered the building of 31 forts to guard the country's coastal ports and keep a lookout for invaders. The forts were armed with heavy cannons able to sink enemy ships.

In 1511, Henry's fleet had the world's largest warship, measuring 160 feet long.

Marriage troubles

Henry VIII had hoped that the annulment of his marriage to Catherine of Aragon would mark the end of his marriage problems. In fact, they were only just beginning. Henry would be the most married monarch ever to rule England.

◀ Anne Boleyn was married to Henry VIII for just over three years.

ANNE BOLEYN

Henry married Anne Boleyn in 1533. She gave birth to a daughter, Elizabeth, later that year, and it was hoped that a son would follow. In fact, Anne was pregnant three more times in the next three years, but none of the babies survived. On May 2, 1536, Anne was arrested and accused of having affairs with other men. She and the men were executed, although there was little evidence that they were guilty.

JANE SEYMOUR

Even before Anne Boleyn was arrested, Henry had started seeing a young noblewoman named Jane Seymour. They were married two weeks after Anne's execution and, the following year, Jane gave birth to Henry's son and heir, Edward. Unfortunately Jane fell sick with a fever and died just 12 days after the birth.

◀ Jane Seymour, the king's third wife.

ANNE OF CLEVES

Distraught after the death of Jane Seymour, Henry let Thomas Cromwell arrange a marriage that would be politically useful. Cromwell chose Anne, daughter of the Duke of Cleves from what is now Germany. Henry agreed after seeing a portrait of Anne, but when they met, he did not like her. The marriage went ahead in 1540, but within a year it had been annulled. Anne was given a pension and outlived Henry by 10 years.

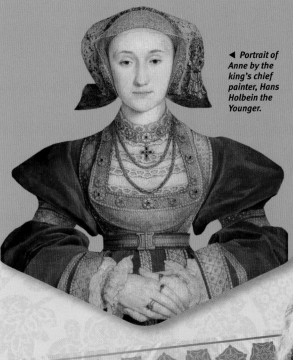

◄ Portrait of Anne by the king's chief painter, Hans Holbein the Younger.

CATHERINE HOWARD

In the spring of 1540, Henry fell in love with the 19-year-old Catherine Howard, a cousin of Anne Boleyn. They married in July 1540. In the summer of 1541, it was revealed that Catherine had had several boyfriends before meeting the king, and had continued seeing them after her marriage. Henry was furious, and Catherine and the men were executed for treason.

▲ Catherine Howard, also painted by Holbein.

◄ Catherine Parr, the king's final wife.

CATHERINE PARR

Catherine Parr had been married twice when she met Henry in 1542. Both her husbands had died, so she was free to marry the king in July 1543. Catherine persuaded Henry to bring his daughters Mary and Elizabeth back to Court and to recognize them as heirs if Edward had no children. After Henry died, Catherine married an old friend, Sir Thomas Seymour. She died in childbirth in 1548.

The sick king

The young Henry was a tall, muscular man who was rarely ill and enjoyed athletic sports and boisterous play. As he grew older, however, he became seriously ill and obese.

THE YOUNG HENRY

About 6 foot tall, Henry VIII was a skilled sportsman. He would spend many hours each day riding, hunting, or playing tennis. He was particularly fond of jousting—a form of fighting on horseback using long, blunt spears called lances.

▶ *One of the suits of armor Henry would have worn during jousting competitions.*

Henry as a young man.

JOUSTING FALL

On January 24, 1536, Henry's horse fell during a joust and rolled on top of him. He was unconscious for more than two hours and suffered severe head and leg injuries. His left leg had a deep ulcer which constantly wept pus and blood and wouldn't heal. Within a few weeks, painful sores had spread to his right leg. Riding was impossible

His wives may have disagreed, but Henry jousted wearing the motto "True Heart."

THE HEAD WOUND

The head injury he suffered in 1536 was serious, but Henry seemed to recover well. But then he began suffering from headaches and violent mood swings, and became suspicious of people around him. Modern doctors think this personality change might have been caused by brain damage.

MALARIA

When Henry was 30 years old he fell sick with a severe fever that left him weak and exhausted. Modern doctors think this may have been malaria. The fever returned several times over the years.

▶ Too much food and a lack of exercise saw Henry grow very fat in his later years.

FINAL DECLINE

In the final months of his life, Henry was so fat and his legs so painful that his doctor had a wheeled carriage made so that he could be moved around his palace. It is said that the scent of congealed pus from his leg ulcers was so bad that people could smell Henry coming before he entered a room. Henry died in 1547, aged just 55.

The "Rough Wooing"

Mary, Queen of Scots
(1542–1587)

Henry wanted his son, Edward, to marry Mary, Queen of Scots. The Scottish nobles did not want their child-queen to marry an English prince, so they refused permission. Henry responded by declaring war. This became known as the "Rough Wooing."

QUEEN OF SCOTS

Mary was just six days old when she became Queen of Scotland following the death of her father, James V, in 1542. Her cousin, the Earl of Arran, became regent and made a deal with Henry that Mary would marry Edward in ten years time. England and Scotland would remain separate kingdoms until a child of Mary and Edward inherited the two thrones.

EDINBURGH ON FIRE

When the Scottish parliament rejected the marriage deal, Henry sent an army under Edward Seymour, Duke of Somerset, to invade Scotland in May 1544. He captured Edinburgh and burned the entire city to the ground. Seymour could not capture the castle, so he left Edinburgh and marched back to Berwick, burning every town he passed.

ANCRUM MOOR

In February 1545, the Earl of Angus led an army against an English force near the Scottish city of Jedburgh. The two armies met on Ancrum Moor. The Scots managed to lure the English into a disorganized attack, then launched their own tightly disciplined assault. Nearly half the English army was killed or captured.

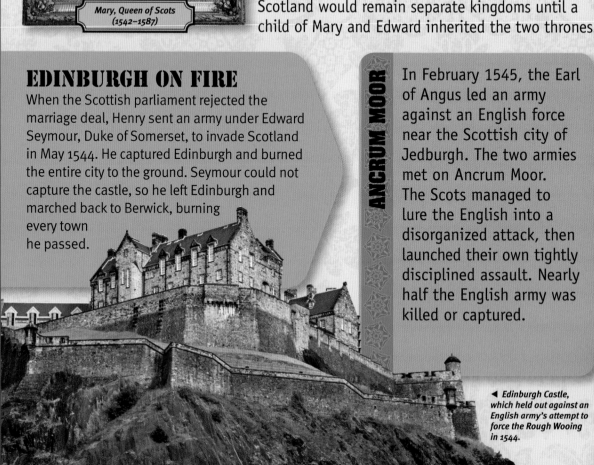

◀ Edinburgh Castle, which held out against an English army's attempt to force the Rough Wooing in 1544.

The succession crisis

As Henry became increasingly ill, he started to plan the future of the Tudor dynasty. His marriage problems had caused confusion over which of his children were legitimate and who would succeed him to the throne.

HENRY'S WILL

Once he accepted that he was dying, Henry wrote a will. This repeated the **Succession** Act, but added that if Elizabeth died without children the throne should then go to the Grey family—the children of Henry's younger sister Mary. The grandchild of his other sister Margaret was not mentioned—she was Mary, Queen of Scots.

◄ *St George's Chapel, Windsor Castle, where Henry VIII is buried.*

THE SUCCESSION ACT

Parliament passed an act in 1544 written by Henry naming Prince Edward as the heir to the throne. If Edward died without producing children, the throne would then pass to his elder sister, Princess Mary, daughter of Catherine of Aragon. If she also died without children the throne would then go to Princess Elizabeth, daughter of Anne Boleyn.

► *Holbein's portrait of Edward as a young child.*

THE COUNCIL OF REGENCY

Henry's will named 16 noblemen and government officials who were to act as a Council of Regency until Edward, then only nine years old, became an adult. The will also named another 12 men who could advise the council but did not have a vote in reaching decisions.

Before Henry VIII, there were no formal rules about who should inherit the crown.

1547–1553

Edward VI: the reformer

The new King Edward VI was a firm supporter of the Protestant faith. Although only a boy, Edward asked his government to introduce strict Protestant reforms. He also favored nobles who were Protestant and gave them top jobs. But Edward's policies would soon cause trouble.

THE ENDVR
WORDE ETH
OF THE FOR
LORD EVER

SVPERSTITION

IDOLATRY

ALL FLESHE
IS GRASSE

FEYNED
HOLINE

DELAYED ANNOUNCEMENT

Henry VIII died on January 28, but the noblemen with him decided to keep this a secret to ensure a smooth succession. His uncle, Edward Seymour, brother of Jane, brought the new King Edward VI to London, while another noble collected Princess Elizabeth. Both were brought to the Tower of London and given an armed guard. Only then was the death of Henry announced.

◄ *An imagined scene showing the handover of power from Henry in his deathbed to his son, Edward. The figure of the pope lies on the ground, symbolizing the end of papal authority in England.*

KEY EVENTS

February 4, 1547	**1549**	**March 24, 1550**	**January 22, 1552**
Edward Seymour is made lord protector, ruling on behalf of Edward (see page 46).	Rebellions break out over Protestantism and enclosures (see pages 48–49).	A treaty ends the "Rough Wooing" war with Scotland (see page 47).	Seymour is executed and replaced by John Dudley (see page 50).

When Edward was six months old, his father built him a new home—Nonsuch Palace.

THE BOY KING

Edward VI was only nine years old when he became king. Because he was so young, England was governed by a council of 16 noblemen during his reign, according to the terms set down in Henry VIII's will. Edward Seymour soon became leader of the council and lord protector—effectively ruling in Edward's place—awarding himself the title of Duke of Somerset.

Edward VI (1537–53)

BACKLASH

Edward's strong support for the new Protestant Church would lead to rebellions by supporters of the old Catholic faith in 1549. Another uprising caused by unemployment and changes to land law took place in East Anglia. Both were put down amid much bloodshed.

PROUDLY PROTESTANT

Edward encouraged Archbishop Cranmer, the Archbishop of Canterbury, to write a new Book of Common Prayer to be used in all church services in England. The book remains the basis for Church of England services to the present day.

EDUCATION

Edward VI established and reformed a number of schools during his short reign, including one in Stratford-upon-Avon, which is believed to have been attended in later decades by William Shakespeare.

▶ *Edward VI School in Stratford-upon-Avon still stands today.*

July 6, 1553
Edward dies, naming his cousin, Lady Jane Grey, as his successor (see page 52).

February 12, 1554
Jane is queen for just nine days before being overthrown and executed by Mary I (see page 53).

The king's government

◀ The Seymour family coat of arms.

Early in Edward's reign, Edward Seymour, the lord protector, only had the authority to call meetings and lead discussions. Within two months, however, he had gained so many powers that he was virtually as powerful as a king.

EDWARD SEYMOUR

Henry VIII had made Seymour the Earl of Hertford and the commander of his army against the Scots. His skill as a soldier made him popular, as did his charm. Unfortunately, when he became lord protector, he also showed himself to be greedy and dishonest.

RUTHLESS REGENT

When his younger brother Thomas was found to be plotting to grab power, Seymour ordered his execution. Another noble was sacked from the government simply for asking a question that Seymour did not like.

▶ Thomas Seymour, who was sentenced to death by his own brother, Edward Seymour, in 1548.

War in Scotland

The Rough Wooing war against Scotland that had begun under Henry VIII continued under Edward VI. It was to see butchery and massacre, but the English couldn't force through the wedding.

BATTLE OF PINKIE CLEUGH

Edward Seymour gathered a large number of troops and marched into Scotland, defeating the Scottish army at Pinkie Cleugh in 1547. From there, the English army marched across southern Scotland, seeking to break the will of the Scottish nobles and force them to allow Mary, Queen of Scots to marry Edward VI.

MARY FLEES

In 1548, King Henri II of France offered to send an army to help the Scots if Mary was allowed to marry a French prince. The Scottish parliament agreed. In August, Mary left for France. The French army arrived to inflict a defeat on the English.

▶ Mary was hidden at Inchmahome Priory after Pinkie Cleugh.

◀ Fa'side Castle was burned down by the English before the Battle of Pinkie Cleugh, killing everyone inside. It was rebuilt in the late 16th century.

THE WOOING ENDS

Once Mary was safely in France, the English accepted there was little point in continuing to try to bully Scotland into a marriage. A treaty signed in 1550 saw all English troops leave Scotland.

At the Battle of Pinkie Cleugh, two thirds of the Scottish army was killed or captured.

The Prayer Book Rebellion

In 1549, the Church of England introduced the Book of Common Prayer, setting out the new form of Protestantism favored by Edward VI. Officials were sent out to force everyone to use it. Rebellion followed.

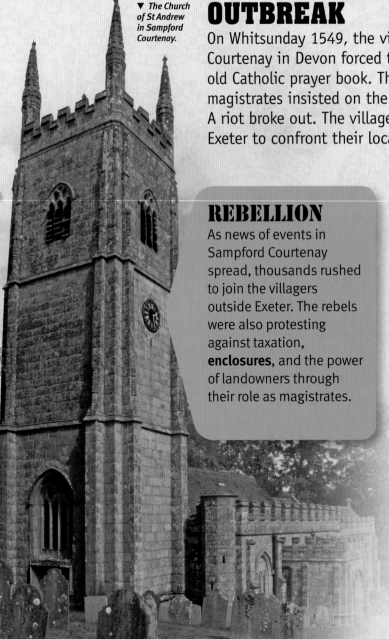

▼ The Church of St Andrew in Sampford Courtenay.

OUTBREAK

On Whitsunday 1549, the villagers of Sampford Courtenay in Devon forced their priest to use the old Catholic prayer book. The following Sunday, magistrates insisted on the use of the new book. A riot broke out. The villagers then marched to Exeter to confront their local bishop.

REBELLION

As news of events in Sampford Courtenay spread, thousands rushed to join the villagers outside Exeter. The rebels were also protesting against taxation, **enclosures**, and the power of landowners through their role as magistrates.

DEFEAT

The rebels laid siege to Exeter for five weeks, but they were eventually defeated. Their leader, Humphrey Arundell, was captured and executed along with hundreds of the rebels.

▼ A stone memorial marks one of the battles of the rebellion.

PRAYER BOOK REBELLION 1549
⚔ FENNY BRIDGES ⚔

HERE IN THIS MEADOW, ON 29TH JULY 1549 MEN FROM CORNWALL AND DEVON FOUGHT AND DIED TO PRESERVE THEIR RELIGIOUS FAITH AND PRACTICE AND THE LANGUAGE IN WHICH THEY HAD BEEN BROUGHT UP.

OMMA YN DHOL-MA, AN 29NS MYS GORTHEREN 1549, KERNOW HA DEWNANS A OMLADHAS HA MERWEL RAK MENTENA AGA FYTH HAGA USADOW CRYJYK HA'N YETH MAY FYENS-Y MEGYS.

ERECTED 2000 BY THE HONITON HISTORY SOCIETY AND KESKEROW KERNOW WITH HELP FROM LOCAL COUNCILS AND SOCIETIES AND THE ROAD CONTRACTORS

In 2007, the Bishop of Truro issued an apology for the bloodshed of the rebellion.

Kett's Rebellion

As the Prayer Book Rebellion was ending, another rebellion broke out in East Anglia. This new revolt aimed to overturn many of the social and economic changes that were taking place.

ENCLOSURES

In medieval times, the farmland around a village was divided up each year so that each family got an equal share. During the Tudor period, much of this land was permanently divided into "enclosures" with the lord of the manor getting more than anyone else.

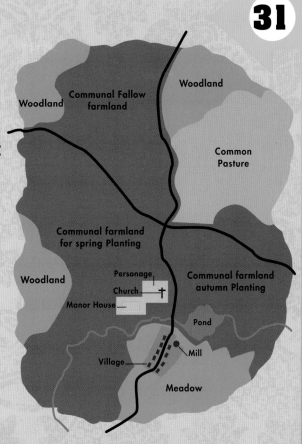

▲ *Map showing communal farmland surrounding a medieval village. In Tudor times, much of this land was enclosed for private use by rich nobles.*

Map labels: Woodland · Communal Fallow farmland · Woodland · Common Pasture · Woodland · Communal farmland for spring Planting · Personage · Church · Manor House · Communal farmland autumn Planting · Pond · Mill · Village · Meadow

OUTBREAK

A rebellion began on July 8 when villagers in Hethersett, Norfolk, tore down fences. The landowner, Robert Kett, agreed with the rebels and helped take down his own fences.

▶ *Robert Kett led a movement to tear down fences. He set up camp under an oak tree just outside Norwich.*

KETT'S OAK

By late July, 30,000 men had flocked to Kett's cause. On July 22, Kett stormed Norwich, defeating a government army. John Dudley, Earl of Warwick, was sent in with a large army, which destroyed the rebel forces after three days of bitter fighting. Kett was hanged for treason.

More than 300 people were hanged for taking part in Kett's Rebellion.

A new government

The expensive wars and rebellions that took place during the early part of Edward VI's reign caused Edward Seymour to lose popularity. Soon a new government was in power, but it faced many of the same old problems.

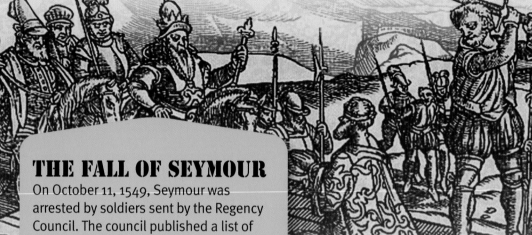

THE FALL OF SEYMOUR

On October 11, 1549, Seymour was arrested by soldiers sent by the Regency Council. The council published a list of alleged crimes committed by Seymour. After a short period in prison, Seymour was released. But in 1552, he was caught plotting a return to power and was executed for treason (as shown in the above picture).

THE RISE OF DUDLEY

In February 1550, John Dudley became the new leader of the Regency Council. Dudley was given the title of Duke of Northumberland by King Edward. Unlike Seymour, he did not try to make himself as powerful as a king, but aimed to organize a government by agreement.

▲ John Dudley

CUTTING COSTS

When Dudley took over, he found that government spending was about $500,000 per year but income was only about $215,000. He cut military spending and sold the city of Boulogne to France for around $260,000, though England retained Calais. By 1553, spending and income were about equal.

◄ During Edward VI's reign, the silver content of coins was reduced to stretch the Crown's dwindling reserves.

In 1545, Dudley introduced tactics that made England's navy one of Europe's most powerful.

POLICY OF PEACE

In 1551, France went to war with the Holy Roman Empire. Both sides appealed to England for help. Dudley refused to go to war, instead sending ambassadors to try to arrange a peace treaty. The move failed, but England remained on good terms with both.

◄ The powerful Holy Roman Emperor Charles V ruled much of central and southern Europe.

IMPOSING ORDER

Dudley's government transferred control of the army in each county to new officials called lord lieutenants. They were allowed to recruit small numbers of permanent soldiers in order to stop riots and protests. As a result, there were no more rebellions.

OVERSEAS TRADE

Dudley encouraged English merchants who wanted to trade with distant lands. He allowed voyages to West Africa and Morocco, even though Spain thought that it should control the trade with those countries. He arranged for the government to pay for voyages of exploration.

RELIGIOUS DISPUTES

King Edward and Thomas Cranmer, Archbishop of Canterbury, both wanted to push on with radical Protestant changes to the Church of England. Worried that they might spark new rebellions, Dudley blocked some of the reforms.

THE POOR LAW

Now that the monasteries had closed, caring for the poor had become a serious problem. Dudley introduced a law that forced each parish priest to register a list of those too poor to care for themselves and another of those rich enough to donate money. The rich in each parish then had to pay to help the poor.

► The poor and the elderly were housed in almshouses such as this one in Coventry.

The king grows up

When King Edward VI was 14, he began to play a role in the government of his kingdom. Edward was not yet allowed to make decisions by himself but his views were increasingly important.

THE COUNCIL OF STATE

From 1551 onward, Edward had weekly meetings with the chief government officials to discuss policy. They were organized by John Dudley. Edward made his views known, but the officials usually followed Dudley's advice.

▲ *The coat of arms given to Dudley when he was made the Duke of Northumberland.*

SAVING THE POUND

The merchant Thomas Gresham was asked to give Edward advice on finances. Within a few months, the English pound became a trusted currency again after years of devaluation by the government. By 1553, the king had no debts at all.

◄ *Edward VI restored the country's finances.*

THE FINAL CRISIS

In January 1553, at age 15, Edward fell ill and, by June, it was clear he was dying. He had no children, so he drew up a succession document. To stop his Catholic half-sister, Mary, succeeding him, he named his cousin, Lady Jane Grey, as queen.

Lady Jane Grey

Lady Jane Grey (1537–54)

In Henry VIII's reign, it had been agreed that if Edward died childless, he would be followed by his half-sisters, Mary and then Elizabeth. But Edward picked Lady Jane Grey instead, although many people wanted Mary as queen.

LADY JANE GREY

Grey was the granddaughter of King Henry VIII's younger sister, Mary. Born in 1537, she was just 16 years old when Edward VI died on July 6, 1553. Shortly beforehand she had married John Dudley's son. Like Edward, she was a Protestant.

NINE-DAY QUEEN

On July 10, at the Tower of London, Jane was declared queen by Dudley, who then left to arrest Princess Mary. But much of the public supported Mary. On July 19, the **Privy Council** met. Deciding Jane's claim to the throne was weak, it declared Mary to be queen, and ordered Jane's arrest.

JANE'S FATE

In September, Jane and her husband were found guilty of treason and sentenced to death. At first, Queen Mary allowed them to live comfortably in a prison. But when a rebellion broke out against Mary, she ordered them both to be executed.

▼ Lady Jane Grey was executed on February 12, 1554.

At her trial, Lady Jane Grey was offered a choice of being burned alive or beheaded.

1553–1558

Mary I: turning back the clock

Mary I came to the throne at a time when England was at a religious crossroads. Protestantism was growing, but was not yet firmly established. Christian Europe was divided in the face of attacks from the east by the Ottoman Empire, but was not yet defeated. Mary decided to put her own fiercely Catholic mark on these turbulent events.

PEOPLE POWER

Mary was swept to power on a wave of public support. She promised peace and prosperity. But before long, she had become massively unpopular by enforcing Catholicism and ordering hundreds of executions. England endured numerous wet summers during her reign, which led to flooding and famine in some parts of the country.

▶ *Queen Mary shortly after coming to the throne in 1553.*

Mary apparently said, "When I am dead... you shall find Calais lying in my heart."

KEY EVENTS

October 1, 1553
Mary is crowned queen, (see page 56).

July 25, 1554
Mary marries Philip II of Spain (see page 57).

September 1554
Mary is believed to be pregnant, but no child is born (see page 57).

1556
Mary seizes land in Ireland to establish English colonies (see page 61).

TRADE

Despite Mary's marriage to the Spanish king, Spain refused to share its lucrative trade routes to the Americas with England. The Anglo-French War of 1557–59 also hit commerce. At the same time, Mary began policies of sponsoring exploration and government reforms that years later would prove to be beneficial to England.

THE LOSS OF CALAIS

Mary married Philip II of Spain and tried to get England to support Spain in its European battles. The English nobles objected as they wanted peace and trade with Europe. Eventually Mary declared war on France, but lost. In 1558, the French captured Calais, England's last possession on mainland Europe. Mary's foreign policy was a failure.

▼ *A 19th-century depiction of France's capture of Calais, England's final French territory.*

BLOODY MARY

Within a few years of her death, Mary had been nicknamed "Bloody Mary" due to the number of people she had ordered to be executed. In all, 283 people were killed for being Protestants —most of them were burned at the stake—and around 1000 fled abroad.

▶ *The former Archbishop of Canterbury, Thomas Cranmer, being burned at the stake as a heretic during Mary's religious persecutions.*

Path to the crown

When Princess Mary was born, nobody thought she would be Queen of England. Henry VIII was expected to have a son who would become king. Her route to the throne was complex and dangerous.

A TROUBLED TEENAGER

Born in 1516, Mary had a happy childhood, but by the time she was a teenager, it was clear that her father wanted to get rid of her mother, Catherine of Aragon, and marry a new wife, Anne Boleyn. Mary was deeply affected by her parents' split and suffered bouts of depression and sickness.

▲ Jane Seymour persuaded Henry to bring Mary back to Court.

BANISHED

When Henry's marriage to Catherine was annulled, Mary was stripped of her royal honors and sent away from Court. After the execution of Anne Boleyn, the 20-year-old Mary returned to Court. However, Mary remained a firm Catholic, leading to arguments with her equally pro-Protestant brother, Edward, when he became king.

TO THE THRONE

Lady Jane Grey ruled as queen for just a few days before she was overthrown in July 1553. Mary then entered London at the head of a procession of 800 nobles and gentlemen. Any Catholics who had been imprisoned by Edward were released.

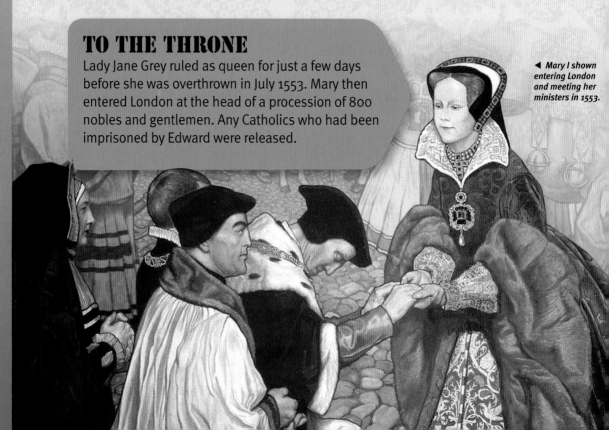

◄ Mary I shown entering London and meeting her ministers in 1553.

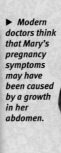

The Spanish marriage

Mary was 37 years old when she became Queen of England. Her first priority was to get married and produce an heir to the English throne.

PHILIP II OF SPAIN

Mary married the Catholic Philip Hapsburg, eldest son of Charles V, the Holy Roman Emperor and King of Spain. But strict conditions were imposed by Parliament. Philip was given the title King of England, but had no power to do anything without Mary's approval. England could not join in any foreign wars unless Parliament agreed.

▲ Upon the death of his father in 1556, Philip II became king of Spain.

WAITING FOR A BABY

In early 1554, Mary showed signs of being pregnant, with the baby due to be born in the summer. However, no baby was born and the signs of pregnancy ended. Mary never had a baby, which meant that when she died, her Protestant sister, Elizabeth, became queen.

► Modern doctors think that Mary's pregnancy symptoms may have been caused by a growth in her abdomen.

WYATT'S REBELLION

The marriage to Philip was unpopular with Protestants, and with those who feared England would be relegated to being a province of the Hapsburg Empire. In January 1554, a Kentish landowner named Thomas Wyatt raised a force of 4000 men and marched on London. Wyatt was defeated by Londoners loyal to Mary. Wyatt and 90 others were executed.

Philip of Spain had 62 different titles, ranging from king and duke to lord and knight.

The return to Rome

At their first meeting, Mary spoke Spanish while Philip replied in French.

When Mary came to the throne she promised that her subjects could practice whatever faith they wanted. Within weeks, however, she began the process of forcing Catholicism on England that would earn her the nickname of "Bloody Mary."

▶ A 19th-century painting showing Hugh Latimer (with the white beard) and Nicholas Ridley (to his right) being led to their execution.

MARY'S FAITH

Mary was a firm Catholic who saw the pope in Rome as head of the Christian Church. In September 1553, she arrested several leading Protestant churchmen, including Thomas Cranmer, the Archbishop of Canterbury. Many other Protestant clergy fled abroad. Mary sacked all clergy who objected to the return of Catholicism.

HERESY AND EXECUTIONS

Mary introduced heresy laws that made it illegal for people to preach religious ideas that disagreed with the pope. Death was the penalty for failing to take back these ideas. The first execution took place on February 8, 1555, when a Cambridge University lecturer was burnt alive for preaching that the pope was mistaken. More prominent victims followed, including the bishops Hugh Latimer and Nicholas Ridley in October.

► At the stake, Thomas Cranmer stated that he was still a Protestant.

CRANMER

Archbishop Cranmer was put on trial for heresy in 1555. He admitted everything, but denied that his words amounted to heresy or treason. He was found guilty and condemned to death. After months of torture, Cranmer broke down and admitted he was guilty. This meant he was free to go, but Mary ordered his execution anyway.

CARDINAL POLE

In 1554, Cardinal Reginald Pole, a great nephew of Edward IV, arrived in England as the pope's official. Two years later he became Archbishop of Canterbury and joined Mary's attacks on Protestantism. But he later pardoned some Protestants and tried to reduce the number of executions.

► Cardinal Pole died just a few hours after Mary.

CALLS FOR A NEW POLICY

In all, 227 men and 56 women were executed for heresy during Mary's reign. Protestants called her "Bloody Mary" and several Catholics thought she went too far. Even Alfonso de Castro, the religious adviser to Philip II of Spain, urged her to stop the executions in case they provoked a revolt. Mary ignored all advice and continued with her extreme policies.

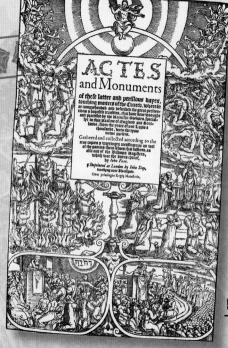

► The title page of Foxe's Book of Martyrs, which describes many of those killed under Mary I.

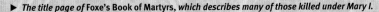

The Irish question

For centuries, the rulers of England had claimed to reign over Ireland as well, though in fact they had little power over the country. Now Mary was determined to impose her rule on the island.

THE KINGDOM OF IRELAND

In 1541, Henry VIII had himself declared King of Ireland, a new title. He then ordered all Irish lords to surrender their titles, on condition that Henry gave them straight back again. In practice nothing changed, but it did mean that Irish lords would now be guilty of treason if they fought against the English king.

THE PALE

Although Mary used the title "Queen of Ireland," her officials ruled only an area around Dublin known as the Pale. It contained many English settlers. Beyond the Pale, Ireland was ruled by lords, some from English families, though most were Irish. Some lords accepted English rule, others did not.

KEY

- Area controlled by English monarch
- Queen's County (English settlers)
- King's County (English settlers)
- Controlled mostly by Irish lords

0   60 miles

0   100 kilometres

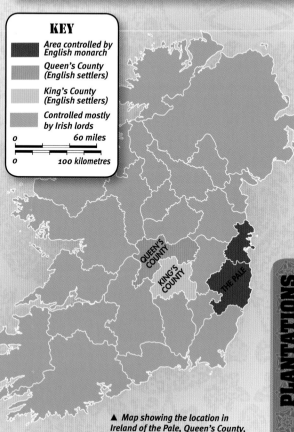

▲ Map showing the location in Ireland of the Pale, Queen's County, and King's County, the areas ruled by the English monarch.

PLANTATIONS

In 1556, Thomas Radclyffe came to Ireland as lord lieutenant to rule the island on behalf of Mary. He dispossessed the powerful Irish O'Moore clan of their land and declared that the area was now to be two counties ruled according to English law: King's County and Queen's County.

BREHON LAW

Most of Irish society was still ruled by Brehon Law, a set of traditional laws that governed marriage, inheritance, land ownership, business, and compensation for injuries. There were frequent disputes about inheritances.

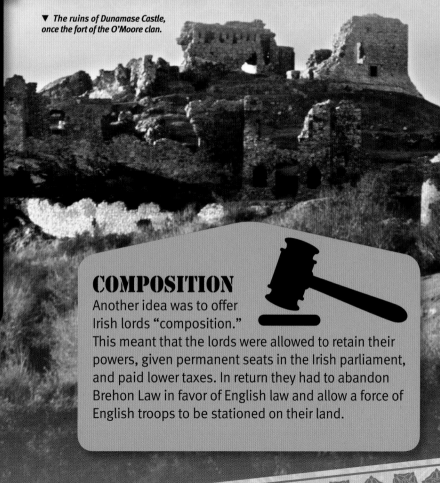

▲ Henry Sidney, Lord Deputy of Ireland under Elizabeth I, sets out from Dublin Castle.

▼ The ruins of Dunamase Castle, once the fort of the O'Moore clan.

SENESCHALS

Mary attempted to impose her rule on Ireland by introducing "seneschals"— military commanders who lived in castles with a strong military force. Using their armies, they had the task of imposing order and stopping feuds. In some areas the system worked, but elsewhere the seneschals caused more trouble than they ended.

COMPOSITION

Another idea was to offer Irish lords "composition." This meant that the lords were allowed to retain their powers, given permanent seats in the Irish parliament, and paid lower taxes. In return they had to abandon Brehon Law in favor of English law and allow a force of English troops to be stationed on their land.

ELIZABETHAN IRELAND

After Mary died, her successor, Elizabeth I, forced Irish lords to accept composition, confiscating lands if they refused. In 1595, the most powerful Irish lord, Hugh O'Neill of Tyrone, announced that he was going to drive the English out of Ireland. He was defeated by 1607 and English government was imposed across Ireland.

▲ Facing arrest, Hugh O'Neill of Tyrone fled to Spain in 1607.

61

1558–1603

Elizabeth I: Good Queen Bess

When Elizabeth became queen, she had the support of nearly everyone. She promised to bring peace, stop religious **persecutions**, and end poverty. The weather even improved, leading to large harvests and a growing economy. But Elizabeth did not get all she wanted. Foreign wars almost led to a Spanish invasion, the economy faltered, and there were numerous plots against her.

PEACE AT HOME

Elizabeth made great efforts to make England peaceful. She produced a new religious policy that avoided extreme Protestantism or Catholicism. She also made efforts to improve the economy. Although most people accepted Elizabeth's rule, a small number of Catholics plotted to kill her.

RELIGIOUS POLICY

In 1558, England was once again a troubled kingdom. Although the government had been well run under Mary, her intolerant religious policy had led to massive unrest. Elizabeth set out to solve the religious problems of England.

◀ *Queen Elizabeth I, painted around 1575.*

KEY EVENTS

November 17, 1558
Elizabeth becomes queen (see page 62).

January 10, 1559
Philip II proposes to Elizabeth, but is turned down (see page 65).

May 8, 1559
Elizabeth is made head of the Church of England (see page 67).

April 10, 1563
Elizabeth disbands Parliament for three years (see page 68).

FOREIGN WARS

Elizabeth tried to avoid wars as they cost money. But in 1585, she sent English troops to aid Protestant Dutch cities against the Catholic Spanish. Philip II of Spain retaliated by sending the Spanish Armada to invade England in 1588. The Armada was defeated, but war lasted for the rest of Elizabeth's life.

▶ The queen talks to her troops before the expected invasion of the Spanish army in 1588.

THE POOR

Towards the end of Elizabeth's reign, the economy declined, increasing the number of poor people. The government passed laws to help them avoid starvation. Three attacks of plague caused thousands of deaths, but overall health improved, as did standards of education and housing.

DRAMA

The latter part of Elizabeth's reign saw a great increase in the production of plays and other theatrical works. Troupes of actors toured the country putting on performances, and several large theaters were built in London. The playwrights of the age, such as William Shakespeare and Ben Jonson, became famous, writing plays that drew large audiences.

◀ The queen was an admirer and supporter of Shakespeare's plays, attending several performances.

February 8, 1587
Elizabeth executes her cousin, Mary, Queen of Scots (see page 69).

August 5, 1588
England's navy defeats the Spanish Armada (see pages 72–73).

March 24, 1603
Elizabeth dies; the crown passes to James VI of Scotland (see page 74).

July 25, 1603
James VI of Scotland is crowned James I of England, ending the Tudor dynasty (see page 75).

Becoming queen

In 1536, when Elizabeth was only three years old, her mother, Anne Boleyn, was executed. Elizabeth was declared to be illegitimate and no longer an official member of the royal family. She would know poverty and danger before she became queen.

INTERROGATION

After Henry VIII's death, Elizabeth lived with her stepmother, Catherine Parr, and Parr's new husband, Thomas Seymour. In January 1549, Seymour was arrested and charged with plotting to marry Elizabeth and overthrow the government. After interrogation, Elizabeth was found innocent, but Seymour was executed.

◀ *Elizabeth I in her coronation robes patterned with Tudor roses.*

ACCUSED OF TREASON

When Wyatt's Rebellion broke out against Queen Mary in 1554, Elizabeth was arrested and imprisoned in the Tower of London. She knew several of the noblemen linked to the rebellion. Although Catholic noblemen argued for her execution, Mary was worried about a major uprising if Elizabeth died. Instead, she was sent to live under house arrest in Oxfordshire.

QUEEN AT LAST

Elizabeth was set free in 1555. She moved to Hatfield House in Hertfordshire, and stayed away from Court. But on November 17, 1558, Mary died and Elizabeth became queen, launching her back into royal life.

▼ *Hatfield House, where Elizabeth spent much of her time.*

In search of a husband

When Elizabeth became queen, everyone assumed that she would want to get married quickly and produce an heir. But Elizabeth would not be rushed.

OTHER SUITORS

Soon after she became queen, Elizabeth received an offer of marriage from Philip II of Spain, who had been the husband of Mary. He made it clear that the marriage would be a political alliance. When Elizabeth learned that Philip had also approached a French princess, she turned him down. She also turned down offers from Erik XIV of Sweden and Archduke Charles II of Austria.

▲ Erik XIV of Sweden pursued marriage with Elizabeth but was turned down.

ROBERT DUDLEY

The man closest to Elizabeth was Robert Dudley, the son of John Dudley, who had tried to make Lady Jane Grey queen. Elizabeth and Robert were childhood friends and had been imprisoned in the tower together. However, Robert was already married. But he remained a close friend of Elizabeth's.

◀ Robert Dudley, who Elizabeth made the Earl of Leicester in 1564.

Elizabeth was so fond of sweet food that her teeth rotted and turned black.

FRENCH BROTHERS

In 1570, Elizabeth sent ambassadors to propose marriage to Henri, heir to the French throne, but Henri never took the idea seriously. In 1579, his younger brother, Francis, proposed to Elizabeth. However, Elizabeth turned him down as most English nobles objected to her marrying a Frenchman.

◀ Elizabeth's sibling suitors, Francis (left) and Henri, who became Henri III of France.

The Church of England

Throughout the reigns of Henry VIII, Edward VI and Mary I, England had been torn apart by religious disputes. Hundreds of people had been executed for their beliefs. Elizabeth was determined to put an end to the unrest.

ELIZABETH'S FAITH

Elizabeth took part in Catholic rituals while Mary was queen. But when she became queen, it made sense for her to be Protestant—under Catholic law, she would have had to declare herself illegitimate. On the other hand, she seems to have taken seriously plans to marry the Catholic Henri of Anjou.

◀ *This portrait of Elizabeth shows the queen in her early forties.*

ACT OF UNIFORMITY

In 1559, Parliament passed the Act of Uniformity. This laid down that only one form of Christian worship was allowed in England. Everyone had to attend church at least once a week or risk being fined one shilling. In practice, many people did not go to Protestant churches, but the Act did effectively outlaw Catholic services.

Elizabeth caught smallpox in 1562, after which she wore white makeup to cover the scars.

SUPREME GOVERNOR

The 1559 Act of Supremacy made Elizabeth the "Supreme Governor" of the Church in England. She was given all the powers of the head of the Church, but by calling her "Governor" it avoided the question of who really was the head of the Church. Catholics thought the pope was head of the Church and the new title avoided antagonizing them.

▲ The title page of the Bishops' Bible, an English translation of the Bible made during Elizabeth's reign. She sits in the center.

THE MISSING BISHOPS

When Elizabeth came to the throne, there was no Archbishop of Canterbury —Mary's Archbishop had died 12 hours after she did. In 1559, Elizabeth dismissed all the remaining bishops left over from Mary's reign. She then chose new bishops who represented a mix of religious views.

▶ Matthew Parker, Archbishop of Canterbury, produced the Bishop's Bible.

THE 39 ARTICLES

In 1563, the Church in England adopted the 39 Articles of Faith. These set out the official religious beliefs of the Church. The 39 Articles steered a middle path between Catholic doctrine and Protestant doctrine.

▲ A priest hole at Harvington Hall, Worcestershire, built at the end of the 16th century, when it was high treason to be a Catholic priest in England.

ROMAN PRIESTS

After a Catholic plot to kill Elizabeth was discovered, Catholic priests were banned from entering England unless they swore allegiance to the queen. Priests still came to carry out rituals for English Catholics. Many Catholic houses had "priest holes," secret rooms where a priest could hide.

Elizabeth passed a law forcing everyone other than nobles to wear a flat cap on Sundays.

The rise of Parliament

During Elizabeth's reign, Parliament became increasingly influential, though she was usually able to control it for her own purposes.

▲ *Queen Elizabeth I on her throne in Parliament.*

REPRESENTATION

Monarchs could raise taxes only if Parliament agreed. It was the people who paid the taxes—nobles, merchants, and landowners—who sat in Parliament. This was made up of two "houses." The House of Lords included all the lords and bishops. The House of Commons was elected by the richer men in the country— probably about 5 percent of men had the vote. For a law to be valid it had to be approved by the Lords, the Commons, and the monarch.

PARLIAMENTARY BILLS

Any member of Parliament, in the Lords or Commons, could introduce a bill. If it was approved by Parliament it went to the monarch, who could agree to it or veto it. This was a way for nobles or commoners to ask the monarch to change a law, lift a tax, or take some other action. Elizabeth often agreed to a bill if Parliament agreed to a tax.

▲ *Sir Christopher Wray, speaker of the House of Commons in 1571.*

PROROGUE

The monarch could prorogue Parliament, meaning it was disbanded and closed down until it was summoned again. In 1563, Parliament passed a motion asking Elizabeth to nominate an heir to take over in case she died. Elizabeth refused, then prorogued Parliament and did not summon it again for three years.

Mary, Queen of Scots

Mary, Queen of Scots
(1542–87)

Mary became Queen of Scotland when she was just six days old, after her father, James V, died. Her ancestry and subsequent adventures would cause Elizabeth a great deal of trouble, as many Catholics saw Mary as the real Queen of England.

▲ Mary, Queen of Scots at Stirling Castle.

MARRIAGE AND EXILE

Mary married three times: first to Francis II of France, then, following his death in 1560, to the Scottish noble, Lord Darnley, with whom she had a son. When Darnley was murdered in 1567, Mary married the man believed to be his killer, the Earl of Bothwell, so Scottish nobles forced her to abdicate. The new king was James VI, Mary's one-year-old son. Mary fled to England.

CATHOLIC PLOTS

Believed by many Catholics to be England's rightful queen, Mary posed a severe threat to Elizabeth. For 19 years, Elizabeth kept Mary prisoner in various castles and houses. In this time, Sir Francis Walsingham, Elizabeth's spy master, foiled numerous Catholic plots to put Mary on the throne.

▶ Sir Francis Walsingham

EXECUTION

In 1586, Walsingham discovered a plot being organized by a Catholic named Anthony Babington with which Mary was involved. Mary was tried and found guilty in October 1586. Elizabeth hesitated to execute a fellow queen and did not sign the death warrant until February 1587. It was then sent on without her knowledge and Mary was beheaded on the day Elizabeth asked for the warrant back.

Mary was widely suspected of having helped to arrange the murder of Lord Darnley.

The seadogs

In the 1550s, English merchants began to make profits by trading with the new Spanish colonies. But in 1564, Spain banned English ships from its colonies to keep the profits for Spanish merchants. So privateers took matters into their own hands.

▼ A replica of a 16th-century warship of the type used by the era's privateers.

SIR FRANCIS DRAKE

After his ship was attacked by Spaniards without warning, English sea captain Francis Drake swore revenge. He spent the next 20 years as a privateer, attacking Spanish ships and ports. From 1577 to 1580, he sailed around the world and made a fortune looting Spanish ships and towns in the Pacific.

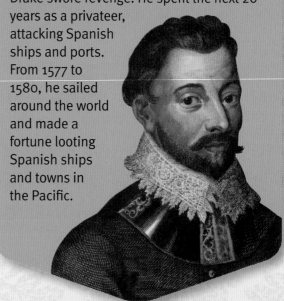

PRIVATEERS

A privateer was a sort of legal pirate—a person, given permission by Queen Elizabeth I to attack and plunder enemy ships and towns in wartime. Some privateers also operated during peacetime.

ELIZABETHAN EXPLORERS

Elizabethan privateers were also known as "seadogs." They included Sir Martin Frobisher, who in 1576 became the first European to meet the Inuit people, and Sir Humphrey Gilbert, who claimed Newfoundland (now in Canada) for Elizabeth I.

The push for trade

During the reign of Queen Elizabeth I, it became clear that large profits could be made trading with distant lands. Merchants set out across the world to make money from commerce.

MERCHANT ADVENTURERS

Elizabethan merchants sailed to new regions looking for wealth and trade. The Muscovy Company was founded in 1555 to trade with Russia and still exists today. The East India Company began in 1600 and soon controlled a vast trade with India. Many other companies were founded, but not all were successful.

▶ *A gold coin from Elizabeth's reign featuring a picture of a ship.*

THE NORTHWEST PASSAGE

Many navigators believed that profits could be made sailing to wealthy China if a route could be found around the top of North America. Several adventurers tried to discover this "Northwest Passage," but nobody could locate an ice-free route.

FINANCIERS

The voyages of trade and discovery were paid for by English financiers. They lent money to the explorers and merchants in return for a share of the profits. Some companies paid the government to give them a monopoly. This meant that they were the only company allowed to trade in a particular way. For instance, the London Merchant Adventurers were the only company allowed to sell English cloth to the Netherlands. Monopolies made high investment worthwhile, but also pushed up prices.

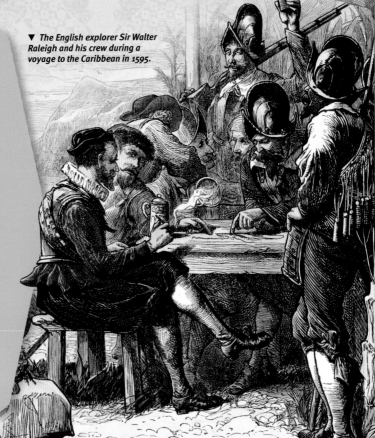

▼ *The English explorer Sir Walter Raleigh and his crew during a voyage to the Caribbean in 1595.*

The Northwest Passage was found in 1850, after centuries of searching by explorers.

The Spanish Armada

By the 1580s, England and Spain were fierce trading and religious rivals. In 1585, war broke out between the two countries when Queen Elizabeth I sent an army to help the Dutch, who were fighting King Philip II of Spain. The king retaliated by sending an enormous fleet, or Armada, to attack England in 1588.

PHILIP'S PLAN

King Philip II's war plan was complex. He told his commander in the Netherlands, the Duke of Parma, to gather an army of 30,000 men. A huge fleet would sail from Spain. First, it would destroy the English fleet in battle. Then, with the country unprotected, it would transport Parma troops across the English Channel to lead the conquest of England.

THE ARMADA

The great fleet that left Spain was made up of 130 ships carrying some 8000 sailors and more than 18,000 soldiers. This Armada was commanded by the Duke of Medina Sidonia, who was a talented soldier but had little experience of sea battles.

▶ Spanish galleons were heavily armed, but slow moving.

THE FLEET

Made up of about 200 vessels, the English fleet was actually larger than Spain's. It was divided in two. Fifty-five ships were in Plymouth waiting for the Armada, while a smaller force was in Dover to stop Parma's army crossing the Channel.

The English ships were smaller and faster than the Spanish galleons.

BATTLE BEGINS

On July 20, the Armada reached English waters. The next day, Drake led the Plymouth ships in an attack, darting between the slower Spanish galleons and bombarding them with gunfire. The Armada managed to escape and, on July 27, took shelter at Calais on the French coast. On the night of July 28, Drake sent six burning ships toward the Armada, which forced the Spanish to scatter into the darkness. The day after, the English fleet pounced on the isolated Spanish ships. Five were destroyed and many others badly damaged. Then a strong south wind drove the Spanish into the North Sea.

THE VOYAGE HOME

In the North Sea, Medina Sidonia decided he could not get to the Netherlands to meet Parma because of the strong south wind. Instead he decided to return to Spain by sailing around Scotland and Ireland. Powerful storms drove many Spanish ships to destruction on rocky shores. In all, only 67 ships and 9800 men got back to Spain.

SCOTLAND

North Sea

IRELAND

ENGLAND

Plymouth   Dover

NETHERLANDS

Calais

FRANCE

SPAIN

▶ *Map showing the route of the Armada's failed attempt to invade England in 1588.*

KEY

Wrecks

Fights in the Channel

Route of Spanish Fleet

0   300 miles

0   500 kilometers

▼ *Packed with easily burnable material, then set alight, an English "fireship" heads into the Spanish fleet.*

The final years

After 1590, Elizabethan England had many problems. Years of poor weather resulted in bad harvests, leaving people hungry and poor. The war with Spain cost a lot of money, so taxes went up and people had even less to spend.

◄ *The Earl of Essex was one of the queen's favorites during the latter part of her reign.*

EARL OF ESSEX

A handsome, talented poet and soldier, Robert Devereux, Earl of Essex, was one of the most popular figures of the 1590s. But in 1599, Elizabeth sacked him after he disobeyed her orders while campaigning in Ireland. In 1601, Essex began a rebellion to overthrow Elizabeth, but nobody joined him. He was executed for treason two weeks later.

GREAT WRITERS

The 1590s saw the start of a golden period in English arts. At this time, great writers such as William Shakespeare and Christopher Marlowe produced plays, while Edmund Spenser and John Lyly wrote poems.

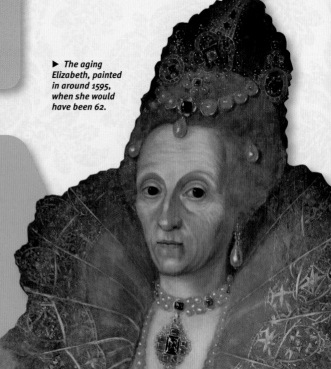

► *The aging Elizabeth, painted in around 1595, when she would have been 62.*

OLD AGE

As Elizabeth passed 60 years of age, she became increasingly weak and ill. Her hair fell out and she grew gaunt and thin. In March 1603, she suddenly collapsed and was taken to her bed. She died quietly several days later.

Toward the end of her life, Elizabeth refused to have any mirrors in her rooms.

The Scottish king

Queen Elizabeth I died childless and there was no obvious heir to the throne. England's nobles held numerous discussions about who the next ruler should be.

THE CONTENDERS

Several people had legitimate claims to the throne, including Henry Hastings, Earl of Huntingdon, the great-great-great nephew of King Edward IV, and the Catholic Princess Isabella Clara of Austria, who was descended from King Edward III. But neither seemed interested in becoming the monarch. Edward Seymour, the nephew of Lady Jane Grey, was also a possible heir, but Elizabeth didn't recognize his claim.

◄ Henry Hastings, the Earl of Huntingdon.

▲ Isabella Clara was happy being the Queen of the Spanish Netherlands and had no desire to become England's monarch.

◄ Nobody disputed James I's right to the crown of England.

THE SCOTTISH CLAIM

King James VI of Scotland was the great-grandson of Margaret Tudor, sister of Henry VIII. His rule of Scotland had impressed England's nobles.

THE SUCCESSION

On the day the queen died, March 24, 1603, a group of nobles declared that Elizabeth had named King James VI to be her successor. A messenger was sent galloping north to tell James to race to London. He left Edinburgh on April 5 and was crowned King James I of England on July 25.

James I had a difficult relationship with Parliament, with constant fights over taxes.

WHO'S WHO?
The Tudor dynasty

This family tree shows every monarch and major member of the royal family from Edward III to James I, the period in which the Tudors reigned for more than a century. Tudor monarchs are marked with a Tudor Rose.

◀ The princes in the tower, Richard (left) and Edward, are parted from their mother by Richard III.

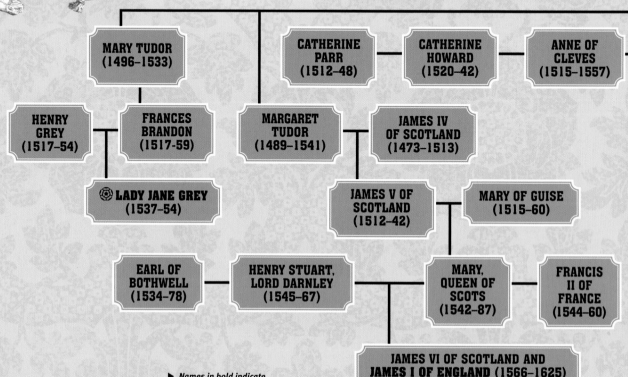

| MARY TUDOR (1496–1533) | | CATHERINE PARR (1512–48) | CATHERINE HOWARD (1520–42) | ANNE OF CLEVES (1515–1557) |

| HENRY GREY (1517–54) | FRANCES BRANDON (1517-59) | MARGARET TUDOR (1489–1541) | JAMES IV OF SCOTLAND (1473–1513) | |

| | LADY JANE GREY (1537–54) | JAMES V OF SCOTLAND (1512–42) | MARY OF GUISE (1515–60) |

| EARL OF BOTHWELL (1534–78) | HENRY STUART, LORD DARNLEY (1545–67) | MARY, QUEEN OF SCOTS (1542–87) | FRANCIS II OF FRANCE (1544–60) |

JAMES VI OF SCOTLAND AND JAMES I OF ENGLAND (1566–1625)

▶ Names in bold indicate monarchs of England and Wales.

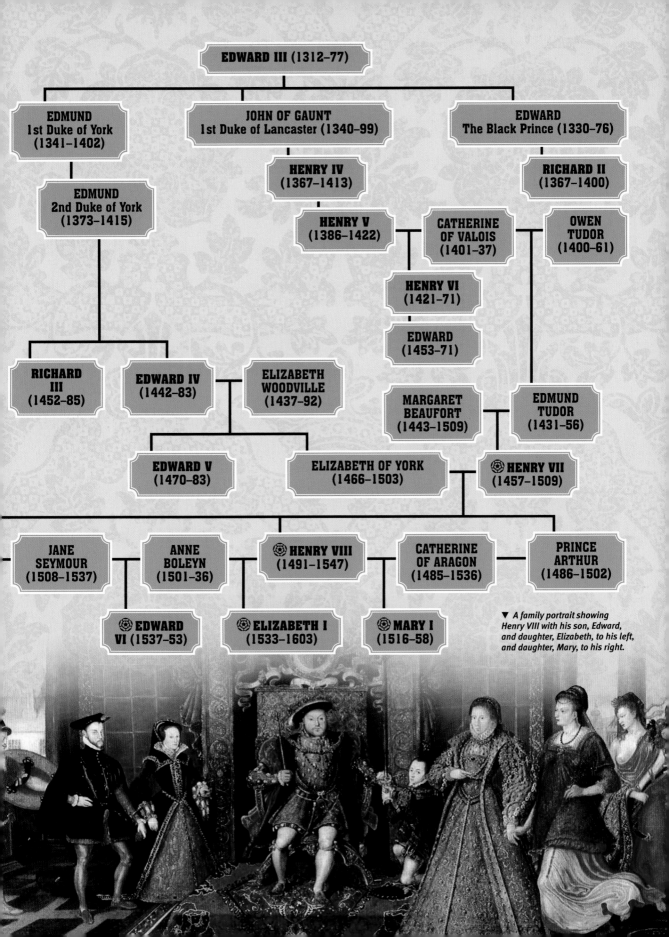

EDWARD III (1312–77)

EDMUND
1st Duke of York
(1341–1402)

JOHN OF GAUNT
1st Duke of Lancaster (1340–99)

EDWARD
The Black Prince (1330–76)

HENRY IV
(1367–1413)

RICHARD II
(1367–1400)

EDMUND
2nd Duke of York
(1373–1415)

HENRY V
(1386–1422)

CATHERINE OF VALOIS
(1401–37)

OWEN TUDOR
(1400–61)

HENRY VI
(1421–71)

EDWARD
(1453–71)

RICHARD III
(1452–85)

EDWARD IV
(1442–83)

ELIZABETH WOODVILLE
(1437–92)

MARGARET BEAUFORT
(1443–1509)

EDMUND TUDOR
(1431–56)

EDWARD V
(1470–83)

ELIZABETH OF YORK
(1466–1503)

HENRY VII
(1457–1509)

JANE SEYMOUR
(1508–1537)

ANNE BOLEYN
(1501–36)

HENRY VIII
(1491–1547)

CATHERINE OF ARAGON
(1485–1536)

PRINCE ARTHUR
(1486–1502)

EDWARD VI (1537–53)

ELIZABETH I
(1533–1603)

MARY I
(1516–58)

▼ A family portrait showing
Henry VIII with his son, Edward,
and daughter, Elizabeth, to his left,
and daughter, Mary, to his right.

GLOSSARY

ACT
A piece of legislation that creates or changes a law.

ANNULMENT
The formal cancellation of a marriage—as if the marriage had never taken place.

ARMADA
A fleet (or group) of warships. The Spanish Armada was a fleet sent by Philip II of Spain to launch an invasion of England in 1588.

CIVIL WAR
An armed conflict between two or more groups within the same country.

CATHOLIC
Relating to Catholicism, or someone who practices Catholicism, a form of Christianity in which the pope in Rome is the head of the Church.

COLONIST
Someone from one country who moves to another country, creating a settlement known as a colony.

CORRUPTION
Engaging in dishonest practices, often for financial gain.

COURT
The building where a monarch lives, as well as the people who live and work there, including family members and ministers.

CROWN
Can be used to describe the symbolic headgear worn by a monarch, the reigning monarch, and the monarch's government.

DIPLOMACY
Conducting political negotiations, often with foreign governments.

DYNASTY
A royal family that produces a series of rulers over several generations.

ENCLOSURE
Fencing off common land for private use.

EXCOMMUNICATE
To banish someone from taking part in Church affairs.

HEIR
The person who will become monarch when the current monarch dies—usually the monarch's eldest son.

HERETIC
Someone who believes something that is against the official beliefs of the Church. Unofficial beliefs are called heresy.

HOUSE
A branch of the royal family.

ILLEGITIMATE
Born outside an official marriage.

LORD CHANCELLOR
In Tudor times, the monarch's most important legal official.

MEDIEVAL
The period of European history from around 600 to 1500 CE.

PARLIAMENT
The official body that represents the people of England and passes laws. In Tudor times, it was made up of the House of Commons (elected officials) and the House of Lords (unelected nobles).

PERSECUTION
Poor or unfair treatment of someone, particularly because of their beliefs.

PRIVY COUNCIL
A small group of senior ministers that advises the monarch.

PROTESTANT
Relating to Protestantism, or someone who practices Protestantism, a form of Christianity that emerged in the 16th century as a reaction against Catholicism. Protestants do not accept the pope as head of the Church.

REFORMATION
An attempt to change the Catholic Church in the 16th century that gave rise to the rival form of Christianity known as Protestantism.

RESTORATION
To return, or restore, a monarch to the throne after they have been deposed.

STATE
An independent nation, or the government of a nation.

SUCCESSION
The sequence, or order, in which people will become monarch.

TRAITOR
Someone who betrays someone or something, such as their country.

TREASURY
The body responsible for managing England's finances.

TREATY
A formal agreement between two or more parties.

UPRISING
A revolt or rebellion against an unpopular law or leader.

WARS OF THE ROSES
A conflict between the English royal houses of Lancaster and York that lasted from 1455 to 1487.

INDEX

Picture credits (t=top, b=bottom, l=left, r=right, c=center, fc=front cover, bc=back cover)

All images public domain unless otherwise indicated:
Alamy.com: 4tl, 17b, 22tr, 25l, 26b, 28t, 33t, 35br, 37cl, 39br, 48l, 49b, 53b, 54cr, 61cr, 61bl, 62br, 64bl, 68bl, 70cl, 71br, 72–73. *Dreamstime*: fc line 1 cl, line 2 cr, line 3 r, line 5 cr, line 6 cl, r, line 7 cl, bc bl, bc line 2 cl, 4br, 5tr, 5bl, 6cl, 7tr, c, 8tr, 10bl, 13b, 14tl, 15c, 16br, 25tr, 26cr, 28tl, 30c, 32br, 34c, 34bl, 36br, 37bl, 42bl, 43cl, 45bl, 45br, 46br, 47tr, 50cr, 53tl, 56tl, 58tl, 58cr, 63br, 64br, 67tr, 69tl, 69cr, 70cl, 71cl, 75cl. *iStock.com*: fc line 1 c, cr, r, fc line 2 l, c, line 3 cl, line 4 cl, r, line 5 l, cl, r, line 7 cr, bc tl, bc line 1 c, line 2 cr, 38cr, 52tl, 57tl, 63tl. *The Mary Rose Trust*: fc line 2 cl, fc line 1 l, cl, 22tr, 37cr. *Shutterstock.com*: 5tr, 8cl, 11tr, 20cl, 30bl. *Wikimedia Commons*: fc line 1 cl Sodacan, fc line 3 l M. Peinado, fc line 3 c NumisAntica, fc line 5 cl Jonathan Cardy, fc line 6 c Alexisrael, 8 br Sodacan, 9b Jdforrester, 10r Sodacan, 13tl Daderot, 15tr Sodacan, 18bl Rasiel Suarez, 20br Basilio, 20tr Katepanomegas and Sodacan, 23b Ludlow Castle, 25b Thomas Duesing, 40–41c Michel Wal, 46tr Socacan, 47b Greig Brash, 50b Classical Numismatic Group, 51br Jim Linwood, 52bl Rs-nourse, 67cl Mum's Taxi, 67 bl QuodVultdeus, 72cl Thyes.

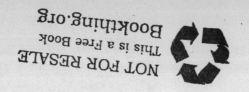
More Praise for *The Day I Stopped Being Pretty*

"*The Day I Stopped Being Pretty* is a shockingly revealing look into the life of a gay black male. The author's candor and exquisite details allowed me the opportunity to learn about a lifestyle I didn't understand. This book is so brutally honest, it had me in tears. Kudos to the author, Rodney Lofton, for telling a story that needed to be told. Thanks to him, my views have changed for the better."

—Tina Brooks McKinney, author of *All That Drama*
and *Lawd, Mo' Drama*

"*The Day I Stopped Being Pretty* chronicles the life of Rodney Lofton from childhood to adulthood where he shares his good times, low times, sexual encounters, relationships and love connections and the acceptance of his sexual orientation. …Coming to the realization that he did not need to seek the love he so desired to receive from his father, author Lofton found that he had the love all the time…in him for he has come to a place where he can love himself."

—Sharel E. Gordon-Love, reviewer, A Place of Our Own (APOOO)
book club

"Author Rodney Lofton brings an in-depth look into the world of male— black male—homosexuality. Baring his soul, he masterfully tells his own personal story of loneliness, depression, and low self-esteem as he sheds light on the lifestyle many choose not to acknowledge. The result is an emotional, heart-tugging, non-fictional work that will require many readers to look and question their own biases."

—Marsha D. Jenkins-Sanders, author of *The Other Side of Through*

"Rodney Lofton makes a stunning debut with his memoir *The Day I Stopped Being Pretty*. He relates his journey from childhood to adulthood in riveting and brutally honest detail. In this page-turner he recounts his struggle in dealing with an emotionally distant father and how it shaped his love relationships. He also shares with the reader his disappointments and triumphs. Lofton's writing style is fluid and it's almost impossible to put this book down. I'm looking forward to further works from this very talented author!"

—Shelley Halima, author of *Azucar Moreno* and *Los Morenos*

"Lofton chronicles his experiences with promising prose, evoking emotion and thought. The issues he addresses as he lays his soul bare for us are still relevant and worth being brought to the forefront once again. Congratulations, Rodney Lofton!"

—Terri Williams, reviewer, Sisters Sippin' Tea Literary Group, Tulsa Chapter, Inc.